DR. Y. BUR...

THE THRONE ROOM

As It Pleases God®

PRAYERS

AS IT PLEASES GOD® MOVEMENT

ASITPLEASESGOD.COM

Send *As It Pleases God* ®

Book Series **and** *Workbook* **Testimonies, Donations, Questions, or Orders to:**

Dr. Y. Bur
R.O.A.R. Publishing Group
581 N. Park Ave. Ste. #725
Apopka, FL 32704
ROAR-58-2316
762-758-2316

"My inmost being will rejoice when your lips speak what is right." Proverbs 23:16

Dr.YBur@gmail.com

Visit Us At:
AsItPleasesGodMovement
AsItPleasesGod

DrYBur.com
AsItPleasesGod.com

Please Donate

Please DONATE to this *Missionable Movement of God* as a GIVE-BACK to the Kingdom. Thanks for your support. Many Blessings.

AIPG Donation Link

Scan to Pay

THE THRONE ROOM
As It Pleases God®

Copyright © 2024 by R.O.A.R. Publishing Group. All rights reserved.

Visit www.DrYBur.com or www.AsItPleasesGod.com for more information. No part of this publication may be reproduced, stored in a retrieval system, or transmitted in any way by any means, electronic, mechanical, photocopy, recording, or otherwise, without the prior permission of the author except as provided by USA copyright law. All rights reserved.

R.O.A.R. Publishing Group
581 N. Park Ave. Ste. #725
Apopka, FL 32704
ROAR-58-2316
762-758-2316
www.RoarPublishingGroup.com

Send Questions or Comments to:
CustomerService@RoarPublishingGroup.com

Published in the United States of America
ISBN: 978-1-948936-95-8
$22.88

ASITPLEASESGOD.COM

AVAILABLE TITLES

ASITPLEASESGOD.COM

Table of Contents

Introduction 9
Throne Room 1 19
   Midnight Prayer 19
Throne Room 2 25
   Detachment of Soul Ties Prayer 25
Throne Room 3 29
   Relational Navigation Prayer 29
Throne Room 4 35
   Activating the Holy Spirit Prayer 35
Throne Room 5 42
   The Casting Down Reversal Prayer 42
Throne Room 6 66
   Lead by Example Prayer 66
Throne Room 7 70
   Hand-to-Finger Approach Prayer 70
Throne Room 8 84
   Heavenly Throne Room Prayer 84
Throne Room 9 88
   Holy Communion Prayer 88
Throne Room 10 95
   Stepping Stones Prayer 95
Throne Room 11 105
   The Cornerstone Prayer 105
Throne Room 12 111
   God's Promises Prayer 111
Throne Room 13 117

Combatting Selfishness Prayer	117
Throne Room 14	121
Healing The Land Prayer	121
Throne Room 15	127
Heaven's Language Prayer	127
Throne Room 16	131
Mental Astuteness Prayer	131
Throne Room 17	135
Newness of Greatness Prayer	135
Throne Room 18	137
Self-Awareness Prayer	137
Throne Room 19	149
Spiritual Fruits Prayer	149
Throne Room 20	159
The Good Shepherd Prayer	159
Throne Room 21	163
Tree of Life Prayer	163
Throne Room 22	171
Unveiling Instincts Prayer	171
Throne Room 23	175
Walking In The Word Prayer	175
Throne Room 24	179
Spiritual Echoes Prayer	179
The Spiritual Seal for the Echoes	182
The Asking the Spiritual Echoe Questions	183
Throne Room References	203

INTRODUCTION

Are you ready to enter The Throne Room: *As It Pleases God*? Are you equipped to develop a *Spirit to Spirit* Connection with your Heavenly Father? Are you prepared to take your Spiritual Relationship with the Holy One to the next level? Are you seeking the INDWELLING of the Holy Spirit? Then again, do you truly understand the POWER hidden in the Blood of Jesus? Well, this book contains prayers that open the Gates of Heaven on your behalf, using the correct approach to the Divine Throne Room of God Almighty, predicated on Revelation 4: The Throne Room of Heaven for a time such as this.

Can one compare a person's personal Throne Room with a Heavenly One? Absolutely! The Heaven on Earth Experience does not discriminate because we are all Spiritual Beings having a human experience. However, we must follow the Divine Instructions to facilitate the Heavenly Experience, *As It Pleases God*.

If we choose not to PLEASE Him, our Heavenly Father, the True Essence of an authentic Throne Room from the Heavenly of Heavens cannot be brought forth in unpalatable conditions that are unpleasing or non-conducive to Him. Suppose we attempt to do so to please ourselves or out of selfishness to control, bully, manipulate, show off, or beat the system. In this

Introduction

case, it will be considered worldly, abominable, and fully yokable from the inside out.

The requirements for gaining access to the Divine Presence of God lie in our approach to all things Spiritual. While at the same time, we often forget that we must follow specific rules of conduct or etiquette PLEASING to Him. When entering to please ourselves, it can unawaringly destabilize the human psyche. So, before moving into The Throne Room Prayers, let us get an understanding first.

The Throne Room of God is a concept found in various Religious and Spiritual Traditions and Practices, symbolizing the seat of Divine Authority and Power. *"The Lord has established His THRONE in the Heavens, and His Kingdom rules over all."* Psalm 103:19.

Nonetheless, for a time such as this and according to the Heavenly of Heavens, The Throne Room: *As It Pleases God* is a SACRED SPACE designed to Plea for Purity, for *Spirit to Spirit* Communion, the unveiling of Divine Purpose, and to download specific information or instructions. Although purity is not perfection, it does not negate the *Spirit to Spirit* Relations needed to set ourselves apart from those who PLEASE God and those who please themselves with Him nowhere in the equation.

Why do we need a Throne Room? We are not required to have one. Still, for the Crème de la Crème from the Heavenly of Heavens, a meeting place is needed but never forced. Historically, the concept of a Throne Room has long been associated with royalty, grandeur, prestige, exclusivity, and power, serving as a symbol of authority, making decisions, and convening with others. Whereas, now, God wants His Divine Throne Room restored, *As It Pleases Him*.

Introduction

The Throne Room of God is described in the Book of Revelation, where the Apostle John provides a vivid account of a HEAVENLY VISION. A vision similar to what we all have had at some point, but fail to remember or recount the details and instructions. Really? Yes, really!

We all received the Blueprinted Instructions before taking our first breath of life; therefore, no one is exempt from having visions. Still, we must PREPARE for them through the envisioning and unveiling process. If not, we will see men walking as trees, similar to the Blind Man of Bethsaida in Mark 8:22-25. What does this mean? We are not seeing people, places, and things correctly, or *As It Pleases God*.

Unfortunately, this is why a lot of Believers are mocked due to their envisioning and discernment faculties being off or keeled. So much so to the point where they call evil good and good evil, who put darkness for light, and light for darkness; who put bitter for sweet, and sweet for bitter, according to Isaiah 5:20. All of which leads to a lot of disappointments and false expectations on our behalf, that of another, and pointing the finger as innocent people get hurt in the interim. Then again, it may cause us to overlook the victims who are secretly or openly terrorized, traumatized, or demoralized to satiate our agendas. Above all, God is calling us out on this matter.

Why are we being called out? The Tears of Heaven are falling to Earth as we sit around twiddling our thumbs without doing our due diligence, *As It Pleases Him*. Or is it that we cannot see the TEARS...or do we think they do not affect us? Well, they do!

Regardless of how we play pretend, the Throne of God for our Heaven on Earth Experience is being left unattended. What does this have to do with us? The Throne Room is often depicted as a place of overwhelming reverence and theological importance in the Eye of God from the Ancient of Days until

Introduction

this very moment. Without reverence, *As It Pleases Him*, we will deem ourselves above Him and approach Him without preparation or authorization as if He owes us something. When, in all actuality, we owe it all to Him!

In this book, The Throne Room: *As It Pleases God*, it serves as the focal point of Heavenly Worship and Devotion, *Spirit to Spirit*. More importantly, this personal place conveys a sense of order, hope, assurance, faith, and justice. Aspiring to partake in the Eternal Glory of the Heavenly Throne renders judgments, pleas, alignments, and decrees for gaining the Divine Attributes to upgrade normal wisdom, understanding, righteousness, and compassion to Supernatural.

Is there a difference between normal and Supernatural? Absolutely! To get to the Supernatural, you must be trained, tested, and approved by the Heavenly of Heavens. Unfortunately, self-appointments will not get it with all things Spiritual. Why? They are Spiritually Guarded!

With every THRONE, there are leaders, followers, loners, shepherds, guards, and wannabees. Now, the question is, which one are you?

As I lead you through each one of the Throne Rooms of Prayers, *As It Pleases God*, you can graduate to the next level when applied correctly according to the Heavenly of Heavens.

Why are there twenty-four instead of twelve Throne Rooms? In the first dispensation of this book, there were twelve rooms. Unfortunately, due to our current status, Mentally, Physically, Emotionally, and Spiritually, God felt as if we needed a little bit more Spiritual Experience in dealing with His Divine Throne Rooms.

Let me explain: The number twenty-four represents harmony, balance, support, and nurturing for purposeful personal growth. The number twelve is associated with completeness, instructions, wholeness, perfection, a sense of

Introduction

harmony, interconnectedness, and Divine Order. To be clear, there is NOT a Spiritual Taboo attached to these numbers. They are Ancient Symbols that convey Spiritual Recognition, Insight, and Significance to those who are connected to the Divine Mission from the Heavenly of Heavens. If one is not connected, *As It Pleases God*, they will miss out on growth, transformation, and restoration designed to take them from where they are to where they need to be according to their Predestined Blueprint.

With this Divine Symbolism, for example, there were twelve Apostles chosen by Jesus, representing the establishment of the early church and the spread of His teachings. Additionally, the Book of Revelation mentions the image of the New Jerusalem as having twelve Gates guarded by twelve Angels, and its walls are said to have twelve foundation stones, each adorned with the names of the twelve Apostles from the twelve Tribes of Israel. Each represents a foundational aspect of the nation, connecting you to them and them to you with information and wisdom hidden in plain sight.

Being that we are engaging in our Heaven on Earth Experiences, for every GATE, we must respect the THRONE guarding it. Without respect, *As It Pleases God*, we can get a Spiritual Padlock, preventing us from possessing what rightly belongs to us or establishing a Divine Cornerstone. Is this fair? Absolutely! Remember this: *"Heaven is my THRONE, and the earth is my FOOTSTOOL."* Isaiah 66:1.

Frankly, we cannot miss what we cannot measure. What does this mean? If we are Spiritually Veiled, we will not realize the Spiritual Padlock, omitted stepping stones, or missed Blessings because the pleasures of life will create a camouflage for the human psyche. Unfortunately, this is why the lust of the eyes, the lust of the flesh, and the pride of life

Introduction

lead to all other malice known to mankind. Blasphemy, right? Wrong! 1 John 2:16 says, *"For all that is in the world—the lust of the flesh, the lust of the eyes, and the pride of life—is not of the Father but is of the world."*

What if there are more things that lead to malice? Once again, they are all derived from these three bonding factors, even if it is inherited in our DNA. How? Conditioning and adaptation lead to more things, even if we do not understand them. Still, they are hidden within our human nature. Thus, we do not know what we would or would not do until we are crushed, tested, or placed under pressure!

In building ourselves from the inside out, each leader has their own set of rules. If you do not learn them, you will become defeated while appearing to win. Why? Your rules will not work on another man's territory, especially when God is nowhere in the equation.

In The Throne Room: *As It Pleases God*, you never enter another man's territory unequipped, unaware, uncharted, or with zero respect. It would be best if you did your homework first. If you do not learn their rules, game, or method of operation…Along with your rules and your game backed up by God's Divine Rules and His Divine Game with a well-developed STRATEGY, *As It Pleases Him*, you are going to be defeated every single time!

What if we are still winning? Winning is a matter of perception. For example, winning in our eyes is not the same as winning in the Eye of God. A selfless Kingdomly Win supersedes an earthly win, especially when selfishness, jealousy, envy, pride, greed, coveting, competitiveness, and rotten fruits are involved.

Now, if you are going to run with the BIG BOYS or GIRLS, you have to learn how to think like them without becoming

Introduction

like them or succumbing to foolery, debauchery, folly, or looking like boo-boo the fool in emotional or mental weakness. How do we make this make sense? For example, in order for a cop to catch a criminal, they must learn how a criminal's mind operates to outsmart or catch them red-handed. And then mastering the ability to decriminalize their minds to avoid getting stuck in a criminal state of being.

The same applies to you...you do not want to walk around naive, aloof, or dumbfounded. There are certain people, places, and things you do not play around with; you must put on your thinking caps regarding your approach, casting down vain imaginations.

How do we decriminalize our mindsets? We must pray, forgive, repent, and use the Fruits of the Spirit. In all simplicity, you must understand your mind, their mind, and God's Divine Perspective with strategic and targeted prayers to till, purge, prune, restore, and cancel. This process gives way to right moves, wrong moves, strategic moves, or unwise moves, and knowing the difference between them all. If not, the psyche can become stuck or trapped in a negative cycle. Then again, you can turn on yourself without knowing it!

The Throne Room: *As It Pleases God* wants you to know that it is time out for the cat and mouse, tit-for-tat games...this is a Theocracy (A GOD RULED NATION). There is a certain order that is set in place, and you need to learn it and pray about it and through it, *As It Pleases God!* Why God's way? No pun intended, but your way is not going to get it in the Eye of God because of your human nature. If you learn the Spiritual Laws of how the Divine System of the Heavenly of Heavens works together for your good, you too, can become SMART...I mean, REAL SMART!

God has created this Universe with Laws, Systems, Strategies, Concepts, and Divine Order, and if you can wrap

Introduction

your head around that, *As It Pleases Him*, WISDOM is yours for keeps!

When we share information without pointing fingers, we can accomplish more than we could ever imagine. When we are able to choose, it gives us the freedom to exercise our minds and think our own thoughts. Trust me; it is hard to go wrong with sharing positive information with options and free will. What does this mean? We do not have to force what we know upon others because it will cause us to become putrid or repulsive in due time.

Knowledge is power, and there is true power in knowledge; however, knowledge without any experience or action changes the rules of the ball game. In order to always keep the ball in our courts, we must understand that learning in action is the key to wisdom, and wisdom is the key to learning while in ACTION.

How is wisdom associated with action, especially when dealing with our Throne Rooms: *As It Pleases God*? First, our brains are wired to make connections, so associating new information with existing knowledge or personal experiences can significantly enhance our ability to remember it, especially when our testimonies are attached. Through personal relevance, storytelling, or empathetic engagement, we give it a deeper meaning, understanding, or connection. Revelation 12:11 seals this fact: *"And they overcame him by the blood of the Lamb and by the word of their testimony, and they did not love their lives to the death."*

Secondly, when taking action, repetition strengthens the neural pathways associated with our memory, making it easier to retrieve, retain, and develop systems of conveyance. When done correctly, *As It Pleases God*, we can unlock our potential to remember and articulate valuable information that touches the hearts of those we interact with, leaving a lasting impact on both ourselves and others. Plus, it helps us

Introduction

to develop magnetic people skills. Proverbs 16:24 says, *"Pleasant words are like a honeycomb, Sweetness to the soul and health to the bones."*

Thirdly, once we engage or take action, our brains process visual data rapidly. More so than sitting around twiddling our thumbs, doing nothing. So, using visual aids, mind maps, rules, or picturesque views can enhance memory retention with triggers or associations. Clearly, this has nothing to do with resting the body; it has everything to do with becoming an active participant in each Throne Room, learning the power of Spiritual Dualism. For this reason, Philippians 2:3 says, *"Let nothing be done through selfish ambition or conceit, but in lowliness of mind let each esteem others better than himself."*

What is Spiritual Dualism? Spiritual Dualism is a concept that suggests the existence of two opposing forces or principles in the world, often represented as good and evil, light and dark, right and wrong, just and unjust, or positive and negative. The Throne Room of real POWER must understand the difference between the two, allowing ourselves time to think, rationalize, and process. Is this not why James 1:19 says, *"So then, my beloved brethren, let every man be swift to hear, slow to speak, slow to wrath."*

Why must a Believer know the differences in Spiritual Dualism? The two forces are in a constant struggle with each other, with an innate desire for balance or warring. Proverbs 11:1 says, *"Dishonest scales are an abomination to the Lord, but a just weight is His delight."* Even if you lack understanding of their presence or authority, it can still affect the psyche, positively or negatively. For this reason, you must build out your prayers, contending or proactively dealing with these factors.

Why do we need to pray? Prayer is a free-will gesture. *"Where do wars and fights come from among you? Do they not come from your desires for pleasure that war in your members?"* James 4:1. Amid all, you must also understand this one fact: *"For we do not wrestle*

Introduction

against flesh and blood, but against principalities, against powers, against the rulers of the darkness of this age, against spiritual hosts of wickedness in the heavenly places." Ephesians 6:12.

If you think this is a joking matter, then keep laughing. But when the joke is on you, your child is in a chokehold and cannot break free, or you need what money cannot buy…you will sing a different tune. The bottom line is that these Throne Room Prayers work, breaking yokes and setting captives free.

Here is the deal: Spiritual Dualism is a fundamental aspect of your belief system, faith, hope, understanding, and desires. All of which influence your understanding of morality, character, the nature of your existence, your ultimate fate, and the fulfillment of your Blueprinted Purpose. 1 Peter 2:11 warns: *"Beloved, I beg you as sojourners and pilgrims, abstain from fleshly lusts which war against the soul." "I say then: Walk in the Spirit, and you shall not fulfill the lust of the flesh."* Galatians 5:16.

The Throne Room: *As It Pleases God* has a Spiritual Language, Vibration, and Frequency connecting you to the Heavenly of Heavens. Then again, it is also designed to bring you into Divine Alignment with who you truly are from the inside out. Therefore, if your Spiritual Language is NOT top-notch, *As It Pleases Him*, you will vibrate on a lower frequency, even when pretending to operate on a higher one.

In this book, the yoke-breaking prayers are designed to help build a Spiritual Foundation that will bring you into a *Spirit to Spirit* Encounter, taking you from where you are into your NEXT. Guaranteed!

So, if you are ready to enter into The Throne Room: *As It Pleases God*, without further ado, let us *"Enter into His gates with thanksgiving, And into His courts with praise. Be thankful to Him, and BLESS His name."* Psalm 100:4.

Throne Room 1

Midnight Prayer

Father, my God, in the Name of Jesus, in the Midnight Hour, I come to You with clean hands and a pure heart, seeking Your Divine Face. As I bow before You, *Spirit to Spirit*, in the stillness of the Midnight Hour, in reverence of You, my Heavenly Father, I seek repentance, forgiveness, and guidance in the dark areas of my life while Divinely Illuminating them through You.

In this sacred moment of the shadowy illuminations of the Midnight Hours, I lay before You all my fears, hopes, desires, and dreams, seeking comfort in Your Divine Wisdom and Loving Hands. Amid this moment of stillness, in the Name of Jesus, renew my assurance of Your unfailing love and calmness as I enter the Divine Veil of Greatness from the Heavenly of Heavens.

The Veil, the Veil, the Veil, I call forth the Holy of Holies in the Name of Jesus, invoking the Divine Presence of the Holy Spirit during this Heavenly Communion process. The Divine Piercing of the VEIL is now upon me; therefore, I come to You for the appropriate Spiritual Alignment and Growth needed to move forward with clarity, courage, renewal, and strength.

With this potent connection to You, *Spirit to Spirit*, I bring forth Divine Intervention and Supernatural Breakthroughs for my Heaven on Earth Experiences. Father, in the Name of Jesus, as You lift the Spiritual Veil on my Mind, Body, Soul,

Midnight Prayer

and Spirit, I surrender to my Divine Blueprint and my reason for being.

In this moment of uninterrupted Spiritual Introspection, Supplication, and Nourishment, I also put on the Whole Armor of God, gearing up for Spiritual Warfare, taking back what the enemy stole from me, and reclaiming territory that rightfully belonged to me.

My Way Maker, through my dedication and commitment to You and the Kingdom, here are my Spiritual Proclamations in this Midnight Hour:

- ☐ I decree and declare that upon my body, the fiery furnace will lose its power, as the communication lines of darkness break over my life, in the Name of Jesus.

- ☐ Lord, forgive me of any sin…I repent and pray that You cleanse my soul as white as snow. Lord, purge me with hyssop of Your glory as You have mercy on my soul in the light of the living.

- ☐ I pray for forgiveness of all of my known and unknown sins as You usher in the Fruits of the Spirit, allowing Love, Joy, Peace, Patience, Kindness, Goodness, Faithfulness, Gentleness, and Self-Control to come forth.

- ☐ When the enemy knocks me down, knocks the wind out of me, sucker punches me, blindsides me, or gets one up on me, REPAIR ME, O Lord, in the Name of Jesus, and cover me with the BLOOD. When I am weak, then I am strong with a comeback that will put my enemy to boot or to shame.

- ☐ Whoever tramples upon the Blood of Jesus that covers me, repair me as they become the STEPPING STONE

Midnight Prayer

for my CORNERSTONE. Clear the way to protect me, O Lord. I am here to do Your Divine Will and follow Your Heavenly Ways, leading Your sheep back to the Kingdom, *As It Pleases You.*

- ☐ In the Name of Jesus, my life must reject any form of wastage. The Blood of the Lamb forbids the enemy from wasting my life, my energy, my resources, or my time without Divine Recompense.

- ☐ Every agenda of the enemy to capture my Spirit Man will fail, in Jesus' Name, as their power fails, creating outages all around them.

- ☐ The Spirit of Poverty and Perverseness, leave my life right now in the Name of Jesus. It is God who has designed me to gain wealth and set me before men in HIGH PLACES. Therefore, I decree and declare my rightful place in my Element of Greatness in the Name of Jesus.

- ☐ To every power tying me down to iniquity, I dethrone their power as You clear them out of my way in the Name of Jesus.

- ☐ I cancel every agenda or projection, trying to cause me to fail. As a result, every form of ill attempt will become my propellant, causing me to succeed at anything that I set out to do, in the Name of Jesus.

- ☐ If I am presently off course or late, reschedule me, in the Name of Jesus. For Divine Timing is my Spiritual Portion, so I lay claim to my BIRTHRIGHT from the Ancient of Days.

Midnight Prayer

- ☐ I denounce any hindering Spirit designed to detour and distract me. By the Blood of Jesus, I bring their plot to a complete halt, binding every debauched thought, plan, or commission into the Pits of Hell until repentance occurs.

- ☐ I bring a refreshed mind to the forefront, allowing me to complete my MISSION, as I anoint the doorpost of the FOUR CORNERS of my brain with the Blood of Jesus, bringing Divine Clarity of Thought and Articulation.

- ☐ I bind the brain fogs clouding my mind, and I bind the hindering Spirit distracting me, rendering it null and void, in the Name of Jesus, casting it into the Pits of Hell.

- ☐ I cut the cord of all brain ties designed to distract me or cause me to forget or lose my train of thought.

- ☐ Every conspiracy against my Divine Destiny or Predestined Blueprint, scatter in the Name of Jesus.

- ☐ Every element of hidden jealousy, envy, pride, greed, coveting, or competitiveness...hear the Word of the Lord: I expose you and expire it in the Name of Jesus.

- ☐ For every door that should be open to me that is blocked, I remove the blockage in the Name of Jesus.

- ☐ Any witchcraft amputation seed designed to detour me or cause any form of backwardness is uprooted and cast into the Pits of Hell with the FIRE of the Holy Spirit on its track.

Midnight Prayer

- [ ] Any buried virtue of mine must be uprooted, as the culprit of this act becomes chaff in the wind. I claim my VIRTUE back to me, demanding restitution because of time lost, in the Name of Jesus.

- [ ] Any strange powers trying to control my DESTINY...I dethrone it with the Blood of Jesus, and I cast it into the abyss from whence it came.

- [ ] Any form of Spiritual Strangulation is cut off and reversed as the Blood of Jesus untangles me, my life, and my DESTINY.

- [ ] Every owner of a load of poverty that is projected on me, Mentally, Physically, Emotionally, Spiritually, or Financially...by Divine Authority from the Heavenly of Heavens, carry your own load! I reject this negative load, for my hands are BLESSED, my basket is BLESSED, and my storehouse OVERFLOWS in prosperity based on my Predestined Blueprint and Spiritual Negev (Underlying Cistern of Divine Provisions).

- [ ] Every owner of ill luck or backwardness, carry your own load as I rebuke it in the name of Jesus. I will only have BLESSINGS, good luck, wealth, prosperity, good success, and forwardness with NO SHAME attached.

- [ ] The anointing that breaks Yokes falls upon my life in the Name of Jesus with the Fire of the Holy Spirit, casting down any and all vain imaginations.

- [ ] Every power anointed to bury my life, you are a liar. I Decree and Declare that this negative forecasting is uprooted and cast into the Pits of Hell from whence it

Midnight Prayer

came. I claim life and vitality in the land of the living, in the Name of Jesus.

In this sacred pause in this Throne Room, *As It Pleases You*, my Heavenly Father, I willfully heighten my *Spirit to Spirit* Connection, Introspection, and Communion with You for valuable opportunities for reflection, guidance, and renewal. For this enduring power of hope and faith, O Lord, I give thanks to You, in the Name of Jesus. Amen.

Throne Room 2

Detachment of Soul Ties Prayer

Father, my God, in the Name of Jesus, I wholeheartedly release the soul ties associated with any unhealthy and toxic relationships, friendships, or unrealistic desires that are not of You. Any form of sin, abuse, debauchery, or manipulation unpleasing to You, I renounce and reject it, them, or that right now in the Name of Jesus. Above all, I release any pain, trauma, confusion, or frustration, breaking free from its power and authority over me, and I command it to leave me now.

Anyone who hurt, negatively influenced, or prevented me from moving on with my life, I bring closure to it, them, or that, without void, error, confusion, or distraction, with love, compassion, and understanding of the place they once held in my Mind, Body, Soul, and Spirit.

I forgive them and myself for any hurt or harm caused, releasing any debt or obligation owed on my behalf or theirs. On this day, in the Name of Jesus, I take possession of all of my Mental, Physical, Emotional, and Spiritual energy expended as my experiences become a stepping stone to my Divine Cornerstone of Greatness.

Lord, I repent of my contributions to any soul tie associated with idolatry, lust, bitterness, or unforgiveness as You lead me to the ROCK that is higher than I. I cut the cord of all of the ties that bind us together as they become dissolved immediately in the Name of Jesus. I free myself from any ill-

Detachment of Soul Ties Prayer

willed or binding energy with power, peace, and authority from the Heavenly of Heavens.

Based upon my Predestined Blueprint and *As It Pleases You* for healing and restoration, I free my heart to love, understand, and trust again with the Blood of Jesus covering the doorpost of my Mind, Body, Soul, and Spirit as the Holy Spirit fills me with His love, peace, and joy, healing any wounds, traumas, or scars that the soul tie has left behind. I Divinely Decree restoration of my identity and purpose in Christ Jesus, doing what You have called me to do.

Father, My God, please help me to avoid any traps or deep-rooted emotional connections designed to ensnare me in another soul tie.

- ☐ In this Throne Room, to *Detach from Soul Ties*, in the Name of Jesus, I am setting healthy boundaries, *As It Pleases You.*

- ☐ In this Throne Room, to *Detach from Soul Ties*, in the Name of Jesus, I am clearly defining my Mental, Physical, Emotional, and Spiritual limitations, *As It Pleases You.*

- ☐ In this Throne Room, to *Detach from Soul Ties*, in the Name of Jesus, I am seeking Divine Guidance in asking the right questions and effectively listening for cues and red flags, *As It Pleases You.*

- ☐ In this Throne Room, to *Detach from Soul Ties*, in the Name of Jesus, I am establishing what is unhealthy for me and my house based on my traumas, sensitivities, or unresolved issues, *As It Pleases You.*

Detachment of Soul Ties Prayer

- [ ] In this Throne Room, to *Detach from Soul Ties*, in the Name of Jesus, I am wholeheartedly listening to my conscience and Spiritual Discernment on when to hold, fold, or walk away when encountering a solid, faulty, weak, or unstable foundation or root to avoid overlooking or underestimating my Divine Blessings or those who are Diamonds in the Rough.

- [ ] In this Throne Room, to *Detach from Soul Ties*, in the Name of Jesus, I seek Divine Intervention on how to love at a distance or with a long-handled spoon without being mean, rude, arrogant, hateful, unkind, or rejecting, *As It Pleases You.*

- [ ] In this Throne Room, to *Detach from Soul Ties*, in the Name of Jesus, I am respectfully building a supportive community of Believers who share Godly Counsel with a healthy perspective, advice, and wisdom about those who are in my life, *As It Pleases You.*

- [ ] In this Throne Room, to *Detach from Soul Ties*, in the Name of Jesus, I am practicing self-awareness, self-control, self-mirroring, and self-analysis to proactively identify soul ties, yokes, or unequally yoked relationships, *As It Pleases You.*

Father, grant me the wisdom to discern the path You have set before me and the strength to walk in it with confidence. Thus, anything or anyone that is not of You, O Lord, must freely find an exit out of my life with the Holy Ghost Fire, clearing the way for the Mate of my Soul.

O Lord, thank you for enabling me to break free from my soul ties. As I detach from them, *As It Pleases You*, I ask for Your peace to fill the void it leaves behind. May your love and grace

Detachment of Soul Ties Prayer

surround me as I move forward in the Spirit of Excellence. As I fully release the yoking connections that kept me bound, I shake the dust off my feet, surrendering all my emotions, memories, and attachments to You for cleansing, purifying, and renewing my Mind, Body, Soul, and Spirit from any lingering effects.

Finally, I ask You to guide me in my future relationships while showing me how to love others and guard my heart, *As It Pleases You.* In Jesus' Mighty Name, I pray. Amen.

Throne Room 3

Relational Navigation Prayer

Father, my God, in the Name of Jesus, as I navigate through the complexities of the relationships in my life, I need You, *Spirit to Spirit*. In this Throne Room of Divine Grace and Mercy, I pray for Your Divine Guidance, Insights, Understanding, and Wisdom for my *Relational Navigational* journey.

In all transparency, it is so easy to become swept up in the allure of a new romance, to become ungrateful, to prioritize material possessions, and to overlook the true values that sustain a meaningful connection, *As It Pleases You*. For this reason, O' Lord, I proactively repent of my ways, asking for Your Divine Mercy, Grace, and Forgiveness.

Above all, in obtaining and maintaining a clean slate, I need Your Divine Assistance in seeing beyond my fleeting attractions and desires with an understanding of the deeper dynamics at play. As I move forward on my journey in the Spirit of Excellence, I pray for the strength and wisdom to exercise discernment in all aspects of my life. Please help me to discern between right and wrong, recognize the choices that align with my values, and have the courage to uphold my integrity and honor to avoid violating my conscience.

In dealing with the matters of the heart, *As It Pleases You*, grant me the insight to recognize when I have placed undue importance on superficial elements like money, physical intimacy, power, or societal status while helping me cultivate

Relational Navigation Prayer

authentic love and understanding instead. Open my mind to the realities of authentic relationships, revealing what may be concealed by my own desires, conditioning, underlying selfishness, or ego.

In this Throne Room of *Relational Navigation*, may this prayer serve as a reminder that true fulfillment in my relationships comes from nurturing genuine connections built on empathy, respect, trust, authenticity, forgiveness, and selflessness. Please guide me on how to be vigilant in tending to the needs of You, my Heavenly Father, *As It Pleases You*. And then, on to tending to the needs of the Kingdom, my Predestined Blueprinted Purpose, myself, my partner, my friends, my family members, and others, fostering growth, unity, peace, and happiness.

Lord, grant me the strength and courage to open up about my struggles for Divine Alignment, *As It Pleases You*. More importantly, in the *Relational Navigational* process, as I seek to make the necessary adjustments, please prevent me from falling victim to unforeseen challenges or traps designed to distract or detour me. As I seek support and wisdom, *As It Pleases You*, I invoke the Spiritual Authority from the Heavenly of Heavens to overcome my obstacles and setbacks, emerging stronger, wiser, and more astute for the Kingdom with no shame attached.

When faced with uncontrollable behaviors or triggers, please help me find the strength to control my negative reactions, thoughts, beliefs, desires, tendencies, perceptions, provocations, and responses. As You guide me toward repentance, forgiveness, and understanding, I invoke the power to refrain from burning bridges, even in challenging situations.

On this day, in my Secret Place, *Spirit to Spirit*, grant me the Divine Wisdom to recognize the types of people to avoid and the discernment to navigate relationships wisely.

Relational Navigation Prayer

I pray for the ability to find the courage and resilience within myself to overcome challenges and not rely solely on external sources for MIRACLES. By the Blood of the Lamb, help me to listen to the voice from within and follow Your guidance in making choices about whom to associate with, whom to avoid, and whom to treat with a long-handled spoon. In doing so, I ask for the strength, discernment, and insight to provide irreplaceable substance in all the relationships that are worth having, keeping, or pursuing, *As It Pleases You*. While simultaneously giving me the desire and know-how to embrace the true love that resides within me and to reciprocate love unselfishly.

As I am in the Throne Room of Your Divine Presence, grant me the Divine Clarity needed to recognize and distance myself from drama, chaos, confusion, debauchery, and negativity that have the potential to hinder my personal growth and progress. Father, my God, in the name of Jesus, as I remove the masks of self-deception, help me to surround myself with supportive, kind-hearted individuals who are committed to building and uplifting.

As I navigate through the complex web of relationships that surround me, I remove the cobwebs in the Name of Jesus, placing everything under the Blood, *As It Pleases You*. As I invoke the Divine Presence of the Holy Spirit to cover this prayer, even in the face of adversity, I bring forth the Spiritual Fruits needed to deal with people on an individualized basis.

Through difficult decisions to stay true to my beliefs and to remain true to You, my Heavenly Father, I understand the importance of choosing relationships carefully and striving to become an asset rather than a liability. In exercising discernment, *As It Pleases You*, I bring forth peace and clarity over my life and those I come in contact with, reflecting goodness, light, and goodwill.

With clarity of mind and heart, grant me the self-awareness to recognize my value and to understand the depth of who I

Relational Navigation Prayer

am while keeping close tabs on my heart posture, *As It Pleases You*. Let me not be swayed by temptation or become misled by external pressures, the issues of life, or the vicissitudes associated. But rather guide me to make choices that reflect goodness, love, oneness, and truth.

As I place my trust in Your Divine Guidance, I ask for the strength to pick up my navigational apparatus and start rebuilding the empire that lies within me. In setting healthy boundaries and foundations for myself in this Divine Throne Room, I commit to upholding Kingdom Standards, *As It Pleases You*, even if I have to forgo enticing opportunities.

With an unwavering commitment, steadfast resolve, and a deep sense of self-respect, I refuse to participate in activities or behaviors that conflict with my values, integrity, and red flags. Nor will I intentionally violate my conscience or bring shame to my name or the Kingdom. If I engage in error or make a mistake without knowing it, please send my internal compass a feeling of discord, an obvious red flag, or a sense of unease to alert my conscience to self-correct or to pay close attention.

I pray for the Divine Wisdom to fully embrace my faith and trust that all things will work together for my good. Help me to recognize and appreciate the BLESSINGS that surround me instead of seeking quick fixes, feeling aloof, or going with a flow that is not of You. Father, with Divine Clarity and Truth, remove the scales from my eyes and open my heart to see the true value of my relationships and the lack thereof. As I seek the courage to face my truths, if I have unawaringly taken anyone or anything for granted, I repent of this behavior, in the Name of Jesus.

My Lord, in my *Relational Navigational* Endeavors, as I become a Source of Light for the Kingdom, I am committed to investing more love, understanding, mercy, and forgiveness in all that I do, say, become, and encounter. Please guide me on how to foster positive bonds to uplift Your sheep with

Relational Navigation Prayer

patience and perseverance, rather than knowingly or unknowingly tearing them down. My Way Maker, if I possess any negative characteristics of impatience, bitterness, hatefulness, abrasiveness, or intolerance in my relations, I cancel them and replace them with lovingkindness.

As the Deep Calleth Unto the Deep, in my *Relational Navigational* efforts, please help me to become open and receptive to the Divine Connections that You bring into my life. In this moment of quiet reflection, I also need the willpower and courage to close the door on what is not of You, remove myself from the fleeting desires of the flesh, and put all of my surface-level comforts under the Blood of Jesus.

Moreover, my Heavenly Father, as I step away from negative influences and relationships, closing the door on them, I need Divine Discernment, *As It Pleases You*. In invoking my Spiritual Birthrights, I place the Holy Spirit at the forefront of my life to filter out or filter through those with malice or debauched agendas. My Lord, this includes anything or anyone designed to distract me from Your Divine Will, including those that do not serve my Predestined Blueprinted Purpose. In addition, I also need Your Divine Assistance in discerning the true intentions of those who cross my path, *As It Pleases You*.

In this Throne Room, as I bow before Your Infinite Wisdom from the Heavenly of Heavens, grant me the Supernatural Strength to cultivate a positive mental attitude on a Divine Level. My Lord, I lay before You all of my known and unknown struggles and doubts that cloud or taint my thoughts, hindering my sense of good judgment or reasoning.

In this surrendering process, whether at peace or when overwhelmed, I am asking for Your Divine Assistance in transforming my negative thoughts, desires, words, and attitudes into positive ones. With the tenacity to believe in myself without being swayed by the opinions of others or the naysayers, I give You all the GLORY.

Relational Navigation Prayer

Above all, in my *Relational Navigational* edifices, may I find the fortification, strength, and valour to let go of unequally yoked people, places, things, situations, events, and behaviors that are counterproductive to the Fruits of the Spirit and my Christlike Character Traits.

In seeking the endless possibilities of Greatness in my relationships with exceptional people skills, *As It Pleases You*, I give thanks. In Jesus' name, I pray, Amen.

Throne Room 4

Activating the Holy Spirit Prayer

My Heavenly Father, I humbly come before You in the Name of Jesus to *Activate the Holy Spirit*. O Lord, may the Divine Presence of the Holy Spirit envelop me in your Divine Love and Tranquility from the Heavenly of Heavens. I am willing and receptive to Your Spiritual Nudges and to recognize when the Holy Spirit is moving and when He is not.

As I transform, *As It Pleases You*, grant me the wisdom, guidance, and inner strength to align my actions, thoughts, words, and beliefs with the Fruits of the Spirit while behaving Christlike. In becoming Spiritually Sensitive, I ask this of You:

- ☐ Holy Spirit, Activate My Spiritual Prophetic Senses...
- ☐ Holy Spirit, Activate My Spiritual Advantage...
- ☐ Holy Spirit, Activate My Spiritual Protocol...
- ☐ Holy Spirit, Activate My Spiritual Satisfaction...
- ☐ Holy Spirit, Activate My Spirit of Illumination...
- ☐ Holy Spirit, Activate My Spirit of Authority...
- ☐ Holy Spirit, Activate My Spiritual Eyes...
- ☐ Holy Spirit, Activate My Spiritual Ears...
- ☐ Holy Spirit, Activate My Divine Intelligence ...
- ☐ Holy Spirit, Activate My Divine Anointing...
- ☐ Holy Spirit, Activate My Spiritual Keys...
- ☐ Holy Spirit, Activate My Spiritual Revelation...
- ☐ Holy Spirit, Activate My Spiritual Inspiration ...
- ☐ Holy Spirit, Activate My Spiritual Bindability...

Activating the Holy Spirit Prayer

- ☐ Holy Spirit, Activate My Spiritual Influence...
- ☐ Holy Spirit, Activate My Spiritual Precision...
- ☐ Holy Spirit, Activate My Spiritual Movement...
- ☐ Holy Spirit, Activate My Spiritual Utterance...
- ☐ Holy Spirit, Activate My Spiritual Quickening...
- ☐ Holy Spirit, Activate My Spiritual Wisdom...
- ☐ Holy Spirit, Activate My Spiritual Righteousness...
- ☐ Holy Spirit, Activate My Spiritual Access to the 12 Gates of Heaven...
- ☐ Holy Spirit, Activate My Spiritual Blueprint...
- ☐ Holy Spirit, Activate My Spiritual Negev...
- ☐ Holy Spirit, Activate My Spiritual Discernment...
- ☐ Holy Spirit, Activate My Spiritual Authority...
- ☐ Holy Spirit, Activate My Divine Elevation...
- ☐ Holy Spirit, Activate My Divine Power...
- ☐ Holy Spirit, Activate My Spiritual Leverage...
- ☐ Holy Spirit, Activate My Spiritual Four Corners...
- ☐ Holy Spirit, Activate My Divine Table...
- ☐ Holy Spirit, Activate My Divine Timing...
- ☐ Holy Spirit, Activate My Spiritual Trumpet...
- ☐ Holy Spirit, Activate My Divine Peace...
- ☐ Holy Spirit, Activate My Divine Prosperity...
- ☐ Holy Spirit, Activate My Divine Awakening...
- ☐ Holy Spirit, Activate My Divine Calling...
- ☐ Holy Spirit, Activate My Spiritual Gifts...
- ☐ Holy Spirit, Activate My Spiritual Fruits...
- ☐ Holy Spirit, Activate My Spiritual Covering...
- ☐ Holy Spirit, Activate My Divine Authenticity...
- ☐ Holy Spirit, Activate My Divine Helpers...
- ☐ Holy Spirit, Activate My Spiritual Voice...
- ☐ Holy Spirit, Activate the Power of Love Within Me...
- ☐ Holy Spirit, Activate My Tongue to Become a Pen of a Ready Writer...
- ☐ Holy Spirit, Activate My Divine Purpose...
- ☐ Holy Spirit, Activate My Divine Passion...

Activating the Holy Spirit Prayer

- ☐ Holy Spirit, Activate the Work of God in my Life...
- ☐ Holy Spirit, Activate My Spiritual Presence...
- ☐ Holy Spirit, Activate My Spiritual Gratefulness...
- ☐ Holy Spirit, Activate My Spiritual Innovation...
- ☐ Holy Spirit, Activate My Spiritual Imagination...
- ☐ Holy Spirit, Activate My Spiritual Originality...
- ☐ Holy Spirit, Activate My Spiritual Inventiveness...
- ☐ Holy Spirit, Activate My Spiritual Resourcefulness...
- ☐ Holy Spirit, Activate My Spiritual Ingenuity...
- ☐ Holy Spirit, Activate My Spiritual Artistry...
- ☐ Holy Spirit, Activate My Spiritual Vision...
- ☐ Holy Spirit, Activate My Spiritual Inspiration...
- ☐ Holy Spirit, Activate My Spiritual Productivity...
- ☐ Holy Spirit, Activate My Spiritual Expressiveness...
- ☐ Holy Spirit, Activate My Spiritual Foresight...
- ☐ Holy Spirit, Activate My Spiritual Pioneering...
- ☐ Holy Spirit, Activate My Spiritual Intuition...
- ☐ Holy Spirit, Activate My Spiritual Quick-Wittedness...
- ☐ Holy Spirit, Activate My Spiritual Creativeness...
- ☐ Holy Spirit, Activate My Spiritual Cleverness...
- ☐ Holy Spirit, Activate My Spiritual Aptitude...
- ☐ Holy Spirit, Activate My Spiritual Genius...
- ☐ Holy Spirit, Activate My Spiritual Talents...
- ☐ Holy Spirit, Activate My Innovative Thinking...
- ☐ Holy Spirit, Activate My Resourceful Mindset...
- ☐ Holy Spirit, Activate My Outside-The-Box Mentality...
- ☐ Holy Spirit, Activate My Divine Visionary Approach...
- ☐ Holy Spirit, Activate My Divine Imaginative Outlook...
- ☐ Holy Spirit, Activate My Divine Perspective...
- ☐ Holy Spirit, Activate My Spiritually Inspired Mindset...
- ☐ Holy Spirit, Activate My Unconventional Thoughts...
- ☐ Holy Spirit, Activate My Divinely Inventive Attitude...
- ☐ Holy Spirit, Activate My Divinely Creative Aptitude...
- ☐ Holy Spirit, Activate My Heavenly Innovative Spirit...
- ☐ Holy Spirit, Activate My Forward-Thinking Mindset...

Activating the Holy Spirit Prayer

- ☐ Holy Spirit, Activate My Artistic Perspective...
- ☐ Holy Spirit, Activate My Problem-Solving Skills...
- ☐ Holy Spirit, Activate My Trailblazing Mentality...
- ☐ Holy Spirit, Activate My Wise Risk-Taking ...
- ☐ Holy Spirit, Activate My Entrepreneurial Mindset...
- ☐ Holy Spirit, Activate My Wise and Dynamic Outlook...
- ☐ Holy Spirit, Activate My Spiritually Curious Mindset...
- ☐ Holy Spirit, Activate My Groundbreaking Mindset...
- ☐ Holy Spirit, Activate My God-Inspired Perspective...
- ☐ Holy Spirit, Activate My Future-Oriented Mentality...
- ☐ Holy Spirit, Activate My Wise Open-Mindedness...
- ☐ Holy Spirit, Activate My Heavenly Visionary Mindset...
- ☐ Holy Spirit, Activate Wise and Strategic Thinking...
- ☐ Holy Spirit, Activate My Insightful Perspective...
- ☐ Holy Spirit, Activate My Heavenly Playful Outlook...
- ☐ Holy Spirit, Activate My Brainstorming Mentality...
- ☐ Holy Spirit, Activate My Wise Conceptual Thinking...
- ☐ Holy Spirit, Activate My Divinely Ingenious Mindset...
- ☐ Holy Spirit, Activate My Adaptiveness and Positivity...
- ☐ Holy Spirit, Activate My Heavenly and Artistic Flair...
- ☐ Holy Spirit, Activate My Wise and Bold Perspective...
- ☐ Holy Spirit, Activate My Divine Passionate Approach...
- ☐ Holy Spirit, Activate My Originality-Driven Mindset...
- ☐ Holy Spirit, Activate Multiple Streams of Greatness...
- ☐ Holy Spirit, Activate My Divine Obedience...
- ☐ Holy Spirit, Activate My Blessings upon Blessings...
- ☐ Holy Spirit, Activate the Whole Armor of God...
- ☐ Holy Spirit, Activate My Supernatural Supply...
- ☐ Holy Spirit, Activate My Covenant Promises...
- ☐ Holy Spirit, Activate My Strategic Ways of Escape...
- ☐ Holy Spirit, Activate Scissors to Cut Ungodly Cords...
- ☐ Holy Spirit, Activate My Tenacity to Break Yokes...
- ☐ Holy Spirit, Activate My Divine Authority to Bind the Wiles of The Enemy...

Activating the Holy Spirit Prayer

- ☐ Holy Spirit, Activate My Divine Recognition of Traps and Snares...
- ☐ Holy Spirit, Activate My Heavenly Guard Over My Heart...
- ☐ Holy Spirit, Activate My Divine Responsibilities...
- ☐ Holy Spirit, Activate My Divine Authority to Cause Any Fiery Furnace to Lose Its Power...
- ☐ Holy Spirit, Activate My Cornerstone of Greatness...
- ☐ Holy Spirit, Activate My Stepping-Stones...
- ☐ Holy Spirit, Activate My Divine Virtues...
- ☐ Holy Spirit, Activate My Patience and Perseverance...
- ☐ Holy Spirit, Activate My Mental Capacity...
- ☐ Holy Spirit, Activate My Brainial Sustainability...
- ☐ Holy Spirit, Activate My Comprehension Skills...
- ☐ Holy Spirit, Activate My Divine Understanding...
- ☐ Holy Spirit, Activate My Spiritual Know-How and How-To...
- ☐ Holy Spirit, Activate My Divine Declarations...
- ☐ Holy Spirit, Activate My Divine and Hidden Fortunes...
- ☐ Holy Spirit, Activate My Joyfulness and Happiness...
- ☐ Holy Spirit, Activate My Spiritual Wells...
- ☐ Holy Spirit, Activate My Underground Cisterns...
- ☐ Holy Spirit, Activate My Divine Manna from Heaven...
- ☐ Holy Spirit, Activate My Divine Flexibility...
- ☐ Holy Spirit, Activate My Divine Excellence...
- ☐ Holy Spirit, Activate My Spiritual Discretion...
- ☐ Holy Spirit, Activate My Divine Jubilation...
- ☐ Holy Spirit, Activate My Heavenly Language...
- ☐ Holy Spirit, Activate My Divine People Skills...
- ☐ Holy Spirit, Activate My Heavenly Communion...
- ☐ Holy Spirit, Activate My Divine Purity...
- ☐ Holy Spirit, Activate My Divine Dominion...
- ☐ Holy Spirit, Activate My Multiplication Factors...
- ☐ Holy Spirit, Activate My Divine Teamwork Abilities...
- ☐ Holy Spirit, Activate My Spiritual Tilling Capacity...

Activating the Holy Spirit Prayer

- ☐ Holy Spirit, Activate My Spiritual Plowing Skills...
- ☐ Holy Spirit, Activate Divine Reciprocity Measures...
- ☐ Holy Spirit, Activate Divine Seedtime and Harvest...
- ☐ Holy Spirit, Activate My Heaven on Earth Experience...
- ☐ Holy Spirit, Activate My Spiritual Earthen Vessel...
- ☐ Holy Spirit, Activate My Divine Trust...
- ☐ Holy Spirit, Activate My Spiritual Faith and Hope...
- ☐ Holy Spirit, Activate My Spiritual Clearance...
- ☐ Holy Spirit, Activate My Spiritual Shamelessness...
- ☐ Holy Spirit, Activate My Helmet of Salvation...
- ☐ Holy Spirit, Activate My Righteousness Breastplate ...
- ☐ Holy Spirit, Activate My Shield of Faith...
- ☐ Holy Spirit, Activate My Shoes of Peace...
- ☐ Holy Spirit, Activate My Sword of the Spirit...
- ☐ Holy Spirit, Activate My Belt of Truth...
- ☐ Holy Spirit, Activate My Ability to Reverse Negatives into Positives...
- ☐ Holy Spirit, Activate My Ability to Create Win-Wins...
- ☐ Holy Spirit, Activate My Spiritual Repentance...
- ☐ Holy Spirit, Activate My Spiritual Forgiveness...
- ☐ Holy Spirit, Activate My Spiritual Mercy...
- ☐ Holy Spirit, Activate My Divine Unifying Faculties...
- ☐ Holy Spirit, Activate My Spiritual Oneness from Within...
- ☐ Holy Spirit, Activate My Invisible Crown of Greatness...
- ☐ Holy Spirit, Activate My Spiritual Prophet from Within...
- ☐ Holy Spirit, Activate My Spiritual Self-Control...
- ☐ Holy Spirit, Activate My Spiritual Astuteness...
- ☐ Holy Spirit, Activate My Divine Clarity...

Holy Spirit Activate...Activate...Activate...In the Name of Jesus... By The Blood of the Lamb, I Give Thanks to My Heavenly Father... Amen...Amen...and Amen.

Throne Room 5

The Casting Down Reversal Prayer

In the Name of the Father, Son, and Holy Spirit, by Divine Decree, I cast down the Spirit of Disobedience and Disillusionment. I repent for all of my known and unknown atrocities, dealing with the sins of my attitude, thoughts, words, desires, habits, fruits, seeds, deeds, behaviors, and human nature. As I become a work-in-progress to Your Divine Will and Ways, lead me to the ROCK that is higher than I.

In this Throne Room: *As It Pleases You*, I cover myself with the Blood of the Lamb as my Spiritual Atonement from the Heavenly of Heavens. I also reclaim my Spiritual Rights to have my one-on-one, *Spirit to Spirit* Relationship with You, my Heavenly Father.

My Wonderful Counselor, I pray that You pass over me as I seek forgiveness for all of my wrongdoings, as I put away all works of darkness, ill will, idolatry, and debauchery. In a repented state of being, my Everlasting Father, You said that You would never leave me nor forsake me, so I am placing a Spiritual Demand, invoking Divine Redemption and Mercy in the Name of Jesus.

On this day, as I remove the mask of disobedience, I replace it with the Spirit of Obedience, putting away all of my dullness, lukewarmness, and stiff-necked behaviors hindering my *Spirit to Spirit* Relationship with You. In the absolute

The Casting Down Reversal Prayer

victory of my Heaven on Earth Experience, I am persuaded that neither death, nor life, nor angels, nor principalities, nor powers, nor things present, nor things to come, nor height, nor depth, nor any other created thing, shall be able to separate me from Your love in Christ Jesus, my Sovereign Lord.

In reclaiming my Divine Spiritual Power with the full Armor of God, I rebuke the Spirit of Rebellion, ushering in the Spirit of Unity and Oneness, *As It Pleases You*. As I put on the breastplate of righteousness, the belt of truth, the helmet of salvation, and my sandals of peace, I take up the shield of faith and the sword of the Spirit to do what they are designed to do. For this reason, I am forgiving myself and others for dropping the ball on my Spiritual Weapons.

From the Ancient of Days, I come into a Divine Agreement that I am a child of the Most High God from the Heavenly of Heavens. I acknowledge my Royal Lineage as a co-heir with Jesus; therefore, I cast down any form of sickness, deformation, blindness, deafness, muteness, aloofness, or lewdness based on the unmerited favor, mercy, and BLESSINGS that come with my Divine Inheritance.

With Divine Authority from my Merciful Heavenly Father, I remove all the chains or ropes binding or yoking me at the core of my being. By the Blood of Jesus, I break it, break it, break it, as I usher in restoration, wholeness, and healing with a Spiritual Hedge of Protection around me and my family. I come against all darkness, torment, fear, anger, guilt, shame, anxiety, pain, illness, depression, irrational behaviors, and feelings of worthlessness, sending it back to the Pits of Hell from whence it came.

From this day forward, I see my impurities for what they are; I will not deny them, rationalize, justify, deflect, or project them. Lord, I vow to work on them, *As It Pleases You*, using the Fruits of the Spirit, building my character one step at a time, putting away pride, rebellion, unbelief, jealousy, envy, selfishness, ambition, control, self-independence, bitterness,

The Casting Down Reversal Prayer

and self-sufficiency. I will embrace humility, obedience, faith, contentment, selflessness, humility, liberation, dependence, and reliance, *As It Pleases You*.

As my Spiritual Inheritance, I am united as ONE with Jesus. So, I renounce any pain, torment, or iniquities of my Forefathers, marking it with debt paid in full without dabbling or straddling the fence. I cast down these associations, taboos, and yokes, severing ties, replacing them with peace, freedom, and comfort as the Holy Spirit intercedes on my behalf, removing all unjustified, bitter, or venomous inflictions and restoring me to the Kingdom of God.

In this Throne Room: *As It Pleases You*, I am seated with You in the Heavenly of Heavens; therefore, I carry the Divine Authority of Christ Jesus, embracing love, joy, patience, and acceptance of my Divine Inheritance. I also Spiritually Seal the factors of being the salt of the earth to walk in Your Divine Will, according to my Predestined Blueprint, while laying claim to my purity and innocence from the Garden of Eden. It was mine from the BEGINNING of time, and I want it back right now, in the Name of Jesus. Thus, I remove the Spiritual Blinders, deception, and false beliefs, healing my Mind, Body, Soul, and Spirit with NO shame, guilt, or unworthiness attached. In doing so, here are the Divine Reversals:

- ☐ I cast down the controlling Spirit of JEZEBEL, and I replace it with the Spirit of HUMILITY, GOODWILL, and ONENESS.

- ☐ I cast down the Spirit of ABANDONMENT, and I replace it with the Spirit of RELATIONSHIP, STRENGTH, PURPOSE, and DIRECTION.

The Casting Down Reversal Prayer

☐ I cast down the Spirit of ALONENESS, and I replace it with the Spirit of COMPANIONSHIP, SOCIABILITY, and GOOD RELATIONS.

☐ I cast down the Spirit of ANGER, and I replace it with the Spirit of CALMNESS, SELF-CONTROL, KINDNESS, and RATIONALITY.

☐ I cast down the Spirit of ANNOYANCE, and I replace it with the Spirit of HARMONY, JOY, COMFORT, and RELIEF.

☐ I cast down the Spirit of ANXIETY, and I replace it with the Spirit of PEACE, CONTENTMENT, and CALMNESS.

☐ I cast down the Spirit of any DOWNFALL, and I replace it with the Spirit of REDEMPTION, ELEVATION, and ASCENSION.

☐ I cast down the Spirit of ARROGANCE, and I replace it with the Spirit of HUMILITY and KINDNESS.

☐ I cast down the Spirit of BACKWARDNESS, and I replace it with the Spirit of FORWARDNESS, FAVOR, and FORGIVENESS.

☐ I cast down the Spirit of being ABUSED, and I replace it with the Spirit of STRENGTH, WISDOM, TENACITY, FORGIVENESS, FAITH, and COURAGE.

The Casting Down Reversal Prayer

☐ I cast down the Spirit of being ACCUSED, and I replace it with the Spirit of WORTHINESS and PRAISE.

☐ I cast down the Spirit of being ASHAMED, and I replace it with the Spirit of UNASHAMEDNESS, BOLDNESS, and CONFIDENCE.

☐ I cast down the Spirit of being ATTACKED, and I replace it with the Spirit of PROTECTION and SAFETY.

☐ I cast down the Spirit of being BEATEN DOWN, and I replace it with the Spirit of ELEVATION and FORTIFICATION.

☐ I cast down the Spirit of BLINDNESS, and I replace it with the Spirit of VISION, KNOWLEDGE, INSIGHT, and WISDOM.

☐ I cast down the Spirit of being BOSSED AROUND, and I replace it with the Spirit of being THE BOSS with Humbleness of Character.

☐ I cast down the Spirit of being BRUSHED OFF, and I replace it with the Spirit of ACCEPTANCE and ACKNOWLEDGEMENT.

☐ I cast down the Spirit of being BULLIED, and I replace it with the Spirit of COMFORT, VALUE, SUPPORT, ADMIRATION, and SECURITY.

The Casting Down Reversal Prayer

☐ I cast down the Spirit of being BURDENSOME, and I replace it with the Spirit of LIGHTNESS, IMPORTANCE, PURPOSE, and PATIENCE.

☐ I cast down the Spirit of being CHEATED, and I replace it with the Spirit of RECOMPENSE, FORGIVENESS, CALMNESS, WISDOM, PATIENCE, and UNDERSTANDING.

☐ I cast down the Spirit of being CONTROLLED, and I replace it with the Spirit of FREEDOM and SELF-CONTROL.

☐ I cast down the Spirit of being CUT DOWN, and I replace it with the Spirit of being BUILT UP, CHERISHED, and REVERED.

☐ I cast down the Spirit of being CYNICAL, and I replace it with the Spirit of CONFIDENCE and TRUST.

☐ I cast down the Spirit of being DEGRADED, and I replace it with the Spirit of being ELEVATED, UNDERSTOOD, and SUPPORTED.

☐ I cast down the Spirit of being DEHUMANIZED, and I replace it with the Spirit of RESPECT, HONOR, DIGNIFICATION, and COMPASSION.

☐ I cast down the Spirit of being DISRESPECTED, and I replace it with the Spirit of RESPECTFULNESS and APPRECIATION.

The Casting Down Reversal Prayer

- ☐ I cast down the Spirit of being DISTRUSTED, and I replace it with the Spirit of TRUSTWORTHINESS.

- ☐ I cast down the Spirit of being FAKE, and I replace it with the Spirit of ORIGINALITY, GENUINENESS, and CONFIDENCE.

- ☐ I cast down the Spirit of being GOALLESS, and I replace it with the Spirit of AMBITION and GOAL ORIENTEDNESS.

- ☐ I cast down the Spirit of being IGNORED, and I replace it with the Spirit of GOOD ATTENTION.

- ☐ I cast down the Spirit of being INSULTED, and I replace it with the Spirit of STRENGTH, STATURE, and RESPECT.

- ☐ I cast down the Spirit of being INTERROGATED, and I replace it with the Spirit of PEACE, CALMNESS, and STRENGTH.

- ☐ I cast down the Spirit of being INVADED, and I replace it with the Spirit of PRIVACY and RESPECT.

- ☐ I cast down the Spirit of being ISOLATED, and I replace it with the Spirit of being INCLUDED and CELEBRATED.

- ☐ I cast down the Spirit of being JUDGED, and I replace it with the Spirit of POSITIONING.

The Casting Down Reversal Prayer

- ☐ I cast down the Spirit of being LEFT OUT, and I replace it with the Spirit of INCLUSION.

- ☐ I cast down the Spirit of being LIED ON, and I replace it with the Spirit of TRUTH and JUSTICE.

- ☐ I cast down the Spirit of being MISLED, and I replace it with the Spirit of DIRECTION.

- ☐ I cast down the Spirit of being MISUNDERSTOOD, and I replace it with the Spirit of UNDERSTANDING.

- ☐ I cast down the Spirit of being MIXED UP, and I replace it with the Spirit of ANALYZATION, IMPACT, and DECISIVENESS.

- ☐ I cast down the Spirit of being NAIVE, and I replace it with the Spirit of DISCERNMENT and MATURITY.

- ☐ I cast down the Spirit of OBLIGATION, and I replace it with the Spirit of RIGHTNESS OF DUTY.

- ☐ I cast down the Spirit of being OFFENDED, and I replace it with the Spirit of FORGIVENESS, SIGNIFICANCE, FRIENDLINESS, and EVOLUTION.

- ☐ I cast down the Spirit of being SHAMEFACED, and I replace it with the Spirit of REVERENCE.

- ☐ I cast down the Spirit of being STRESSED, and I replace it with the Spirit of CALMNESS and PEACE.

The Casting Down Reversal Prayer

- ☐ I cast down the Spirit of being TARGETED, and I replace it with the Spirit of PURPOSE, FAVOR, and TENACITY.

- ☐ I cast down the Spirit of being TEASED, and I replace it with the Spirit of CALMNESS, CONFIDENCE, and SECURITY.

- ☐ I cast down the Spirit of being UNCOMFORTABLE, and I replace it with the Spirit of COMFORT and GRATEFULNESS.

- ☐ I cast down the Spirit of being UNDERESTIMATED, and I replace it with the Spirit of STRATEGICNESS, TENACITY, and PRECISION.

- ☐ I cast down the Spirit of being UNHEARD, and I replace it with the Spirit of ACKNOWLEDGEMENT, NOTICEABILITY, and UNDERSTANDING.

- ☐ I cast down the Spirit of being UNINFORMED, and I replace it with the Spirit of INFORMATIVENESS and AWARENESS.

- ☐ I cast down the Spirit of being UNKNOWN, and I replace it with the Spirit of being WELL-KNOWN as a good household name.

- ☐ I cast down the Spirit of being UNLOVED, and I replace it with the Spirit of LOVE.

- ☐ I cast down the Spirit of being UNSUPPORTED, and I replace it with the Spirit of GOOD SUPPORT.

The Casting Down Reversal Prayer

- ☐ I cast down the Spirit of being UNWANTED, and I replace it with the Spirit of VALUE, HIGH DEMAND, and IN NEED.

- ☐ I cast down the Spirit of being UPTIGHT, and I replace it with the Spirit of CALMNESS, COOLNESS, and UNDERSTANDING.

- ☐ I cast down the Spirit of being VIOLATED, and I replace it with the Spirit of PURIFICATION to trust life.

- ☐ I cast down the Spirit of BETRAYAL, and I replace it with the Spirit of LOYALTY and STEADFASTNESS.

- ☐ I cast down the Spirit of BITTERNESS, and I replace it with the Spirit of LOVE, FORGIVENESS, PEACE, WHOLENESS, and HAPPINESS.

- ☐ I cast down the Spirit of BLAME, and I replace it with the Spirit of TRUSTWORTHINESS, RESPONSIBILITY, and OWNERSHIP.

- ☐ I cast down the Spirit of BLINDNESS, and I replace it with the Spirit of INSIGHT, VISION, OBSERVABILITY, and WISDOM.

- ☐ I cast down the Spirit of BOREDOM, and I replace it with the Spirit of EXCITEMENT and SHARPNESS.

- ☐ I cast down the Spirit of being BROKEN, and I replace it with the Spirit of HEALING, FORGIVENESS, and RESTORATION.

The Casting Down Reversal Prayer

- ☐ I cast down the Spirit of CLINGINESS, and I replace it with the Spirit of DISENGAGEMENT.

- ☐ I cast down the Spirit of CLUMSINESS, and I replace it with the Spirit of COORDINATION, ATTENTIVENESS, POISE, GRACEFULNESS, and SKILLFULNESS.

- ☐ I cast down the Spirit of CLUTTER, and I replace it with the Spirit of ORGANIZATION, NEATNESS, PROFICIENCY, and MASTERY.

- ☐ I cast down the Spirit of CODEPENDENCY, and I replace it with the Spirit of INDIVIDUALITY, INDEPENDENCE, INTERDEPENDENCY, and HUMBLENESS.

- ☐ I cast down the Spirit of COLDNESS, and I replace it with the Spirit of COMPASSION, EMPATHY, WARMTH, and LOVE.

- ☐ I cast down the Spirit of COMMONNESS, and I replace it with the Spirit of GREATNESS, WISDOM, and UNIQUENESS.

- ☐ I cast down the Spirit of COMPETITIVENESS, and I replace it with the Spirit of TEAMWORK, ASSOCIATION, CONFIDENCE, and HARMONY.

- ☐ I cast down the Spirit of CONFORMITY, and I replace it with the Spirit of INDIVIDUALITY and PURPOSE.

The Casting Down Reversal Prayer

- ☐ I cast down the Spirit of CONFRONTATION, and I replace it with the Spirit of ALLIANCE, UNITY, and RESPECT.

- ☐ I cast down the Spirit of CONFUSION, and I replace it with the Spirit of PEACE and SELF-CONTROL.

- ☐ I cast down the Spirit of CONFUSION, and I replace it with the Spirit of UNDERSTANDING, CLARITY, and HARMONY.

- ☐ I cast down the Spirit of CRITICISM, and I replace it with the Spirit of PRAISE, ADORNMENT, POSITIVITY, and ENLIGHTENMENT.

- ☐ I cast down the Spirit of DEBAUCHERY, and I replace it with the Spirit of HONESTY and UPRIGHTNESS.

- ☐ I cast down the Spirit of DECEPTIVENESS, and I replace it with the Spirit of HONESTY, HUMILITY, and INTEGRITY.

- ☐ I cast down the Spirit of DEFLATION, and I replace it with the Spirit of ELEVATION and SUCCESSION.

- ☐ I cast down the Spirit of DELAY, and I replace it with the Spirit of ADVANCEMENT, TIMELINESS, and PROGRESSIVENESS.

- ☐ I cast down the Spirit of DESTRUCTION, and I replace it with the Spirit of CREATING, CONSTRUCTING, CREATIVITY, and BUILDING.

The Casting Down Reversal Prayer

- ☐ I cast down the Spirit of DISAPPROVAL, and I replace it with the Spirit of APPROVAL and SUPPORT.

- ☐ I cast down the Spirit of DISBELIEF, and I replace it with the Spirit of FAITH, HOPE, and BELIEF.

- ☐ I cast down the Spirit of DISCOURAGEMENT, and I replace it with the Spirit of ENCOURAGEMENT and STRENGTH.

- ☐ I cast down the Spirit of DISGUST, and I replace it with the Spirit of RESPECT, PATIENCE, MERCY, and COMPASSION.

- ☐ I cast down the Spirit of DISTRACTION, and I replace it with the Spirit of PEACE, CONCENTRATION, WATCHFULNESS, and ALERTNESS.

- ☐ I cast down the Spirit of DIVISION, and I replace it with the Spirit of DEVOTION, CONNECTION, LOVE, LOYALTY, and GODLINESS.

- ☐ I cast down the Spirit of DOUBT, and I replace it with the Spirit of CONFIDENCE and COURAGE.

- ☐ I cast down the Spirit of DULLNESS, and I replace it with the Spirit of HUMOR and LAUGHTER.

- ☐ I cast down the Spirit of EMBARRASSMENT, and I replace it with the Spirit of PROUDNESS.

The Casting Down Reversal Prayer

☐ I cast down the Spirit of ENTRAPMENT, and I replace it with the Spirit of DIVINE TIMING.

☐ I cast down the Spirit of EXASPERATION, and I replace it with the Spirit of CALMNESS, CONTENTMENT, and SOOTHABILITY.

☐ I cast down the Spirit of FAILURE, and I replace it with the Spirit of GOOD SUCCESS, ELEVATION, and ASTUTENESS.

☐ I cast down the Spirit of FATIGUE, and I replace it with the Spirit of ENERGETICNESS, SHARPNESS, and EMPOWERMENT.

☐ I cast down the Spirit of FEAR, and I replace it with the Spirit of COURAGE, TENACITY, KNOW-HOW, and FAITH.

☐ I cast down the Spirit of FOLLOWING, and I replace it with the Spirit of LEADERSHIP, SERVANTHOOD, and EXAMPLE.

☐ I cast down the Spirit of FOLLY, and I replace it with the Spirit of WISDOM, UPRIGHTNESS, RATIONALE, and DISCERNMENT.

☐ I cast down the Spirit of FOOLISHNESS, and I replace it with the Spirit of WISDOM, SOUNDNESS, MATURITY, and CAUTION.

The Casting Down Reversal Prayer

- ☐ I cast down the Spirit of FORGETFULNESS, and I replace it with the Spirit of RECALL, ALERTNESS, MINDFULNESS, and WISDOM.

- ☐ I cast down the Spirit of FRUSTRATION, and I replace it with the Spirit of SATISFACTION, GRATIFICATION, CONTENTMENT, and THANKFULNESS.

- ☐ I cast down the Spirit of GREED, and I replace it with the Spirit of SHARING, GOODWILL, and GENEROSITY.

- ☐ I cast down the Spirit of GRIEF, and I replace it with the Spirit of HAPPINESS, HOPE, and FORGIVENESS.

- ☐ I cast down the Spirit of HATE, and I replace it with the Spirit of LOVE, FORGIVENESS, UNDERSTANDING, and CONTENTMENT.

- ☐ I cast down the Spirit of HOSTILITY, and I replace it with the Spirit of FRIENDLINESS and CALMNESS.

- ☐ I cast down the Spirit of HUMILIATION, and I replace it with the Spirit of RESPECT, ENRICHMENT, and ELEVATION.

- ☐ I cast down the Spirit of HURT, and I replace it with the Spirit of HEALING, LOVE, and KINDNESS.

- ☐ I cast down the Spirit of IGNORANCE, and I replace it with the Spirit of AWARENESS, KNOWLEDGE, UNDERSTANDING, and HUMILITY.

The Casting Down Reversal Prayer

- ☐ I cast down the Spirit of IMPATIENCE, and I replace it with the Spirit of PATIENCE, DILIGENCE, WISDOM, and TOLERANCE.

- ☐ I cast down the Spirit of IMPRISONMENT, and I replace it with the Spirit of being SET FREE.

- ☐ I cast down the Spirit of INCOMPETENCE, and I replace it with the Spirit of WISDOM, COMPETENCE, and STRENGTH.

- ☐ I cast down the Spirit of INEFFICIENCY, and I replace it with the Spirit of EFFECTIVENESS, CAPABILITY, and SUFFICIENCY.

- ☐ I cast down the Spirit of INFERIORITY, and I replace it with the Spirit of SUPERIORITY, GENUINENESS, and GOODNESS.

- ☐ I cast down the Spirit of INJUSTICE, and I replace it with the Spirit of JUSTICE.

- ☐ I cast down the Spirit of INSECURITY, and I replace it with the Spirit of CONFIDENCE.

- ☐ I cast down the Spirit of INSIGNIFICANCE, and I replace it with the Spirit of SIGNIFICANCE.

- ☐ I cast down the Spirit of INSTABILITY, and I replace it with the Spirit of STRENGTH, STABILITY, and POISE.

The Casting Down Reversal Prayer

- ☐ I cast down the Spirit of INTIMIDATION, and I replace it with the Spirit of BOLDNESS.

- ☐ I cast down the Spirit of INVALIDITY, and I replace it with the Spirit of FAVOR, POWER, and INFLUENCE.

- ☐ I cast down the Spirit of JEALOUSY or ENVY, and I replace it with the Spirit of CONTENTMENT, GRATEFULNESS, and ACHIEVEMENT.

- ☐ I cast down the Spirit of being LABELED, and I replace it with the Spirit of being SOUGHT-AFTER, APPROVED, and ACCEPTED.

- ☐ I cast down the Spirit of LACK, and I replace it with the Spirit of ABUNDANCE, OVERFLOW, and PROVISION.

- ☐ I cast down the Spirit of LIMITATION, and I replace it with the Spirit of UNLIMITED POTENTIAL.

- ☐ I cast down the Spirit of MALICE, and I replace it with the Spirit of HARMONY and KINDNESS.

- ☐ I cast down the Spirit of MANIPULATION, and I replace it with the Spirit of WISDOM, DISCIPLINE, RESTRAINT, CONFIDENCE, and UNDERSTANDING.

- ☐ I cast down the Spirit of MATERIALISM, and I replace it with the Spirit of CHARITABILITY, CONTENTMENT, and GENEROSITY.

The Casting Down Reversal Prayer

- ☐ I cast down the Spirit of MINIMIZATION, and I replace it with the Spirit of MAXIMIZATION.

- ☐ I cast down the Spirit of MISFORTUNE, and I replace it with the Spirit of FAVOR.

- ☐ I cast down the Spirit of MOCKERY, and I replace it with the Spirit of DISENGAGEMENT and PROTECTION.

- ☐ I cast down the Spirit of NEGATIVITY, and I replace it with the Spirit of POSITIVITY, ENLIGHTENMENT, and UPWARDNESS.

- ☐ I cast down the Spirit of NEGLECT, and I replace it with the Spirit of RESPECT, FORGIVENESS, and LOVE.

- ☐ I cast down the Spirit of NEGLIGENCE, and I replace it with the Spirit of PREPAREDNESS, PROACTIVENESS, and ATTENTIVENESS.

- ☐ I cast down the Spirit of OBNOXIOUSNESS, and I replace it with the Spirit of TOLERANCE.

- ☐ I cast down the Spirit of OPPOSITION, and I replace it with the Spirit of PEACE, COOPERATION, NEGOTIATION, and AGREEABILITY.

- ☐ I cast down the Spirit of OVERSIGHTEDNESS, and I replace it with the Spirit of INQUIRY, DISCERNMENT, and SECOND-SIGHT.

The Casting Down Reversal Prayer

- ☐ I cast down the Spirit of PARANOIA, and I replace it with the Spirit of PRONOIA, where everything works for my good.

- ☐ I cast down the Spirit of PERVERSENESS, and I replace it with the Spirit of MORALITY, INTEGRITY, and RIGHTEOUSNESS.

- ☐ I cast down the Spirit of PETTINESS, and I replace it with the Spirit of UNDERSTANDING, FORGIVENESS, and MINDFULNESS.

- ☐ I cast down the Spirit of POVERTY, and I replace it with the Spirit of WEALTH, PROVISION, and DIVINE ALIGNMENT.

- ☐ I cast down the Spirit of POWERLESSNESS, and I replace it with the Spirit of POWER, OBEDIENCE, and AUTHORITY. .

- ☐ I cast down the Spirit of PROCRASTINATION, and I replace it with the Spirit of READINESS, DILIGENCE, PROMPTNESS, and DETERMINATION.

- ☐ I cast down the Spirit of PUNISHMENT, and I replace it with the Spirit of MERCY, REPENTANCE, FORGIVENESS, and FAVOR.

- ☐ I cast down the Spirit of REBELLION, and I replace it with the Spirit of OBEDIENCE, HUMILITY, and RESPECT.

The Casting Down Reversal Prayer

- ☐ I cast down the Spirit of RECKLESSNESS, and I replace it with the Spirit of WISDOM, CAUTION, DISCERNMENT, and GOOD JUDGMENT.

- ☐ I cast down the Spirit of REGRET, and I replace it with the Spirit of HOPE.

- ☐ I cast down the Spirit of REJECTION, and I replace it with the Spirit of CONNECTION.

- ☐ I cast down the Spirit of RELIGIOUSNESS, and I replace it with SPIRITUALITY, LOVE, and CONNECTION.

- ☐ I cast down the Spirit of RESENTFULNESS, and I replace it with the Spirit of TOLERANCE, PLEASANTNESS, and FORGIVENESS.

- ☐ I cast down the Spirit of REVENGE, and I replace it with the Spirit of FORGIVENESS, PEACE, JUSTICE, and PERFECT TIMING.

- ☐ I cast down the Spirit of RUDENESS, and I replace it with the Spirit of POLITENESS, RESPECT, and COURTESY.

- ☐ I cast down the Spirit of SADNESS, and I replace it with the Spirit of HAPPINESS and JOY.

- ☐ I cast down the Spirit of SCATTEREDNESS, and I replace it with the Spirit of COLLECTIVENESS and FOCUS.

- ☐ I cast down the Spirit of SHYNESS, and I replace it with the Spirit of BOLDNESS, AUTHORITY, and COURAGE.

The Casting Down Reversal Prayer

- ☐ I cast down the Spirit of SLAVERY, and I replace it with the Spirit of LORDSHIP.

- ☐ I cast down the Spirit of SLOTHFULNESS, and I replace it with the Spirit of PROMPTNESS and DILIGENCE.

- ☐ I cast down the Spirit of STUBBORNNESS, and I replace it with the Spirit of RESPECT, FLEXIBILITY, TEACHABILITY, and COOPERATION.

- ☐ I cast down the Spirit of SUFFOCATION, and I replace it with the Spirit of REJUVENATION and NEWNESS.

- ☐ I cast down the Spirit of the fear of being SCARED, and I replace it with the Spirit of TRUST to know that all things will work together for my good.

- ☐ I cast down the Spirit of THIEVERY, and I replace it with the Spirit of JUSTICE and RESTITUTION.

- ☐ I cast down the Spirit of UNATTENTIVENESS, and I replace it with the Spirit of ALERTNESS.

- ☐ I cast down the Spirit of UNCLEANLINESS, and I replace it with the Spirit of PURITY, TIDINESS, AGILITY, and VIRTUOUSNESS.

- ☐ I cast down the Spirit of UNENTHUSIASM, and I replace it with the Spirit of ENTHUSIASM, CREATIVITY, and PASSION.

The Casting Down Reversal Prayer

- ☐ I cast down the Spirit of UNFRIENDLINESS, and I replace it with the Spirit of FRIENDLINESS, CHARITY, and COMMUNITY.

- ☐ I cast down the Spirit of UNGRATEFULNESS, and I replace it with the Spirit of GRATITUDE and GRATEFULNESS.

- ☐ I cast down the Spirit of UNIMPORTANCE, and I replace it with the Spirit of AUTHORITY and IMPORTANCE.

- ☐ I cast down the Spirit of UNPREDICTABILITY, and I replace it with the Spirit of LOGICALITY and WISDOM.

- ☐ I cast down the Spirit of UNRELIABILITY, and I replace it with the Spirit of RESPONSIBILITY and DILIGENCE.

- ☐ I cast down the Spirit of UNREMORSEFULNESS, and I replace it with the Spirit of REMORSEFULNESS, MERCY, and CONCERN.

- ☐ I cast down the Spirit of UNSAFENESS, and I replace it with the Spirit of DIVINE GUIDANCE, PROTECTION, and ILLUMINATION.

- ☐ I cast down the Spirit of UNSURENESS, and I replace it with the Spirit of DECISIVENESS, CLARITY, and UNDERSTANDING.

- ☐ I cast down the Spirit of VAGUENESS, and I replace it with the Spirit of CLARITY, DIRECTNESS, and PRECISION.

The Casting Down Reversal Prayer

- ☐ I cast down the Spirit of VAIN IMAGINATIONS, and I replace it with the Spirit of DIVINE PURPOSE and DESTINY.

- ☐ I cast down the Spirit of VIOLENCE, and I replace it with the Spirit of MEEKNESS, CALMNESS, and PEACE.

- ☐ I cast down the Spirit of WASTEFULNESS, and I replace it with the Spirit of STEWARDSHIP, PRUDENCE, WISDOM, and GRATEFULNESS.

- ☐ I cast down the Spirit of WORTHLESSNESS, and I replace it with the Spirit of WORTHINESS, VALUE, and PRISTINENESS.

With Divine Illumination from the Heavenly of Heavens, I claim light, joy, courage, innocence, honor, pleasure, health, happiness, rational behavior, and feelings of worthiness as my Spiritual Portion, in the Name of Jesus.

Even if I fall short or get wet, I invoke the Spiritual Covering over my life with a Legion of Angels to protect my Blueprinted Mission of my Heaven on Earth Experiences with an unoffendable heart. For this reason, I will not allow the sun to go down on my wrath without releasing its chokehold or penetration, *As It Pleases You.*

As my Spiritual Compass becomes Divinely Calibrated, no weapon formed against me shall prosper. Even if they send it out, it must go down in the Name of Jesus as I cling to this truth, navigating through the complexities of life. Lord, help me to recognize and resist any form of negativity, fear, or doubt that may seek to undermine my faith and confidence in You. May Your Divine Light find a way to Divinely Illuminate

The Casting Down Reversal Prayer

my path, dispelling any darkness or uncertainty that tries to infringe upon my Spiritual Journey.

    Father, as I walk in victory, *As It Pleases You*, with Your Divine Calibration, may my Spiritual Compass always point toward truth, love, joy, peace, and righteousness, enabling me to overcome any challenges that happen to come my way. In Jesus' Name, I pray. Amen.

THRONE ROOM 6

Lead by Example Prayer

Father, my God, in the Name of Jesus, I come before you seeking guidance as I strive to lead in the Spirit of Excellence, *As It Pleases You*. In all holiness, I come before you, seeking your help in demonstrating diligence, integrity, and wisdom in all that I do, say, and become. As You are in the LIGHT, I too, will also walk in the Light in fellowship with others, while *Leading by Example*, as the Blood of Jesus cleanses me on a moment-by-moment basis.

O Lord, guide me in my actions, thoughts, beliefs, and decisions so that I can reflect Your Divine Will and bring Supernatural honor to Your Name and the Kingdom. Grant me strength and understanding to lead in the Spirit of Excellence, always striving to do what is right in Your sight.

As I embark on this journey through life, I am reminded of the profound impact of my attitude. I understand that my attitude is akin to my shadow, an ever-present companion that influences every aspect of my existence. Father, my God, I acknowledge that my attitudes shape my thoughts, emotions, and actions, and they are magnified by my five senses. So, I humbly ask for the strength and wisdom to adopt an attitude that reflects the virtues exemplified by Christ Jesus.

Lord, may my attitude be a beacon of positivity, resilience, and compassion, radiating love and understanding to those around me. Please guide me on how to *Lead by Example*,

Lead by Example Prayer

becoming a source of inspiration and hope in a world that is often clouded by negativity, debauchery, control, and confusion. By the Blood of Jesus, I prune back every dead branch, controlling branch, diseased branch, or devilish branch in my life. Any branch that is not bearing fruit, *As It Pleases You*, I prune it right now...I cut it off, removing all negative attachments, preventing me from bearing good fruit.

In properly governing my Spiritual Fruits, bring to my remembrance everything I need to know with a Supernatural Understanding in conjunction with the Spirit of Wisdom. As You grant me the Divine Discernment to understand the power of my attitude and how to develop a positive mental mindset, *As It Pleases You*, help me to align it with my Predestined Blueprint and Divine Purpose or Passion.

More importantly, I need Your help in recognizing the subtle influence that my attitude has on my words, actions, thoughts, beliefs, and biases that may affect my heart posture and my *Spirit to Spirit* Relations with You.

Amid *Leading by Example*, I dismiss every mind-controlling and negative projection from entities designed to confuse my thought patterns, causing me to lose focus or frustrate me, in the Name of Jesus. Lord, it is written that my enemies shall not rise up or rejoice in their wrongdoings against me because when I fall, I will rise. When I am weak, then I am strong. When I am challenged, I will overcome. By the Blood of the Lamb, they are my stepping stones to my Divine Cornerstone.

Lord, from this day forward, I will not underestimate the significance of nurturing a healthy and virtuous attitude, one that uplifts and edifies both myself and others, even when I do not receive the same in return.

In moments of doubt and difficulty, allow the Holy Spirit to serve as a steadfast Spiritual Anchor, imparting me with the courage and fortitude to overcome challenges and embody the grace and strength of Christ.

Lead by Example Prayer

Father, when *Leading by Example*, I recognize that every decision I make carries a consequence. As I understand and embrace the truth about myself and my reason for being, I invoke the Holy Spirit to help me cultivate positive interactions with myself and others, *As It Pleases You*. In doing so, I pray for the Divine Wisdom, Understanding, and Tenacity to make choices that align with my Divine Purpose, with the clarity to see beyond instant gratification and focus on the long-term impact of my actions.

By becoming a source of encouragement, kindness, and support by Divine Decree, I activate the Law of Reciprocity. When *Leading by Example*, I willfully allow Jesus to go before me, preparing the way with Divine Illumination, making my way safe and prosperous. As the Holy Spirit seeks Divine Opportunities and opens doors that no man can close, I avail myself to receive raises, promotions, bonuses, gifts, surprises, canceled debt, increases, and BLESSINGS, getting rid of the lack or poverty mindset to embrace my Spiritual Negev (Underlying Cisterns of Divine Provision).

Father, help me to recognize the fruits that are falling in and around my life as You grant me the wisdom to make the necessary corrections and to take responsibility for my fruits, whether positive or negative, good or bad, right or wrong. By the Blood of the Lamb, empower me to turn negative outcomes into positive ones and sow them into fertile ground, *As It Pleases You*.

As I come to You with an open heart and a humble Spirit, teach me to focus on doing good deeds, exhibiting authenticity and resilience while encouraging, building, and helping others, *As It Pleases You*, regardless of others' opinions. Grant me the wisdom to discern what PLEASES You and the courage to follow instructions accordingly, putting my feelings and selfishness at bay while building and uplifting myself, those around me, and the Kingdom.

Lead by Example Prayer

In Spiritual Accountability from the Heavenly of Heavens, I come before You, seeking alignment and understanding, *As It Pleases You*. Please help me to correct my way of thinking and level of empathy, guarding my mind against influences that may lead me away from You.

In *Leading by Example*, I invoke the courage needed to overcome the fear of rejection and to let my good deeds speak for themselves. As I cast down the Spirit of Rejection, I usher in the Spirit of Acceptance, Receivability, Approval, Inclusion, Endorsement, Agreement, Support, and Consideration with unwavering authenticity, *As It Pleases You*.

In the Spirit of Excellence, I am committed to embodying Divine Integrity with a Spiritual Compass and Anchor that is already hidden within me. My Father, through Your Divine Love, I am AWARE that I already possess what I need. So, with the diligence needed to move forward in wisdom and humility with my purposeful vision and passion from the Heavenly of Heavens, I PURSUE what rightly belongs to me.

In the Name of Jesus, on this day, I move forward, *Leading by Example* in all thankfulness, respect, honor, and love to my Heavenly Father. Amen.

Throne Room 7
Hand-to-Finger Approach Prayer

By the Hand of God, I invoke the Holy Trinity at the highest level as I meander through life with the Divine Hand of significant power, along with the Heavenly Finger of the Most High.

Life and death are in the power of my hands; therefore, I activate the power of my tongue to eat and reproduce my fruit, *As It Pleases You*. With the *Hand-to-Finger Approach* and *As It Pleases You*, my goal is to bring about conscious awareness, as well as the Divine Revelation regarding the power I possess with what comes out of my mouth and the power I have in my hands.

In this hidden Secret of the Ancient of Days, by the Blood of the Lamb, I maximize the Power of God's Hand and Finger simultaneously while using mine in the Spirit of Oneness.

Father, my God, in the Name of Jesus, You are my refuge and strength, a very present help in trouble and in my time of need. At this moment, as I reach out to You, I now place a Spiritual Demand on Your Divine Hand and Finger to do what You do best. In total surrender, I cannot approach life without You, nor can I have the desire to backtrack or play cleanup. For this reason, I surrender all things, including my messes, mud, scraping the bottom, and ditches, to You.

By Divine Authority from the Heavenly of Heavens, I am using the Power of God's Hand for Spiritual Covering, Guidance, or Empowerment. I am Divinely Invoking Your

Hand-to-Finger Prayer

Divine Hand over my Mind, Body, Soul, and Spirit to regraft, prune, till, heal, restore, or uproot. I will no longer skim over my issues or play patchwork with them as I bring them forth, putting them into their proper perspective, *As It Pleases You.*

- ☐ With the *Hand of God*, I put my SPIRITUAL LIFE into its proper perspective and under the Blood of Jesus, *As It Pleases You*, rebuking and casting down all ill will, debauchery, and any evil eye associated with envy, jealousy, pride, greed, coveting, or competitiveness, in the Name of Jesus.

- ☐ With the *Hand of God*, expose all the ambushments that are hidden to trip me up or cause any form of downfall or shame. Heavenly Father, I come before You to contend against the STRONGMAN SPIRIT that is seeking to hinder, oppress, and cause chaos in my life. I ask for Your Divine Strength and Power to RESIST this Spirit and to overcome its influence, in the Name of Jesus. I pray for Your Heavenly Protection and Deliverance from the hidden and open attacks of the Strongman Spirit or the wolves in sheep's clothing, while always providing me with a way of escape.

- ☐ With the *Hand of God*, I put all of my relationships, friendships, and alliances in their proper perspective and under the Blood of Jesus, *As It Pleases You.* Thus, rejecting all forms of negative energy while interjecting positive energy, in the Name of Jesus, while moving with the Holy Spirit at the forefront, guiding, nudging, and protecting me.

- ☐ With the *Hand of God*, I put my financial stewardship and underlying cisterns in their proper perspective and under the Blood of Jesus, *As It Pleases You.* Anything or

Hand-to-Finger Prayer

anyone illegally holding my possessions, holding them up, or blocking them, I demand their release, in the Name of Jesus. With the backing from the Heavenly of Heavens, I reverse any ungodly blockages and invoke Divine Recompense with clean hands and a pure heart.

- ☐ With the *Hand of God*, I put my career and work in their proper perspective and under the Blood of Jesus, *As It Pleases You*. By the Divine Authority invested in me, I break the yoke and shackles of any setbacks or misalignments hindering my progression, growth, understanding, or lessons, in the Name of Jesus.

- ☐ With the *Hand of God*, I put my physical health and wellness in their proper perspective and under the Blood of Jesus, *As It Pleases You*, as I interject Divine Healing from the Heavenly of Heavens, overcoming the Spirit of Sickness attempting to affect my body. I renounce it as You provide me with the mental, physical, and emotional resilience I need for the Promise of Restoration.

- ☐ With the *Hand of God*, expose those who are around me who are my enemies pretending to be a friend, *As It Pleases You*. You said, 'By their fruits, I will know them.' For this reason, let them be known, in the Name of Jesus, as You develop my Spiritual Eyes to see and my Spiritual Ears to hear the Fruits of the Spirit or the lack thereof. More importantly, do all of this without exposing my Divine Knowledge of who sent them and why they were sent while setting a Spiritual Guard over my mouth as my Spiritual Discernment prevails.

- ☐ With the *Hand of God*, I put my friendships and social connections in their proper perspective and under the

Hand-to-Finger Prayer

Blood of Jesus, *As It Pleases You*. For any ungodly or unpurposeful associations distracting me from Your Divine Will, Purpose, or Blueprint, I kindly release them right now, in the Name of Jesus.

☐ With the *Hand of God*, I put my personal growth and development in their proper perspective and under the Blood of Jesus, *As It Pleases You*. As I Spiritually Till my own ground, I repel all of the cankerworms designed to become a nuisance to my Divine Destiny or damage my reputation. In addition, I repent if I caused cankerworm manifestations due to my disobedience, as restoration is re-established in the Name of Jesus.

☐ With the *Hand of God*, I put my communication and bonding process in their proper perspective and under the Blood of Jesus, *As It Pleases You*. I bring to an end every yoking force distorting my Heavenly Communication in the Name of Jesus. Father, grant me the strength, understanding, and wisdom to overcome any obstacles and silence anything or anyone that prevents me from hearing Your VOICE clearly.

☐ With the *Hand of God*, I put my known and unknown conflicts in their proper perspective and under the Blood of Jesus, *As It Pleases You*. And, whatever is leading me astray or corrupting my Spiritual Home Training, I bring it to a complete halt or resolve, in the Name of Jesus. I pray for Your support and protection as You guide me through life's challenges as I work out my own SALVATION. Amid all, Lord, help me stay connected to Your Divine Wisdom and Unwavering Love for a time such as this.

Hand-to-Finger Prayer

- [ ] With the *Hand of God*, I put my rest, calmness, and relaxation in their proper perspective and under the Blood of Jesus, *As It Pleases You.*

- [ ] With the *Hand of God*, I put my recreational edifices and hobbies in their proper perspective and under the Blood of Jesus, *As It Pleases You.* Lord, unshackle me from a reprobate mind, especially when my mind has strayed from the path of righteousness. My Merciful Father, I seek proactive forgiveness, renewal, and clarity to overcome the negative thoughts and attitudes that have taken root or have become seeded into my mindset. From this day forward, I vow to bring forth a Kingdom Mindset endowed with Divine Wisdom, Understanding, and Know-How.

- [ ] With the *Hand of God*, I put my community involvement and service in their proper perspective and under the Blood of Jesus, *As It Pleases You.* Help me to see the world through Your Divine Lenses as I embrace the value of love, kindness, mercy, and empathy. Thus, I humbly ask for Your HEALING TOUCH on my Mind, Body, Soul, and Spirit, making my people skills impeccable with a positive, lasting impression.

- [ ] With the *Hand of God*, I put my time management and organization in their proper perspective and under the Blood of Jesus, *As It Pleases You.* Any untimely or ungodly entanglements must disentangle me right now, in the Name of Jesus. Lord, as I come to You, my Heavenly Father, with a humble heart and a determined Spirit, I will not be held captive from my Divine Destiny...nor will I allow others to hinder my progress in doing what I have been called to do. Let Your Divine Light shine upon me, illuminating my

Hand-to-Finger Prayer

path, purpose, and passions, taking them from average to Supernatural while empowering me to walk in the Spiritual Direction that You have set for me.

☐ With the *Hand of God*, I put my learning, growth, development, and education in their proper perspective and under the Blood of Jesus, *As It Pleases You*. My Waymaker, I trust in Your Divine Wisdom and Your perfect timing. So, I will not be held captive by my self-imposed or people-imposed limitations as I break out of my little cocoon, doing what I have been called to do in the Name of Jesus.

☐ With the *Hand of God*, I put my forgiveness and reconciliation in their proper perspective and under the Blood of Jesus, *As It Pleases You*. I surrender myself to Your Divine Will for my life, knowing that with Your Everlasting Guidance, I can overcome all obstacles and fulfill the purpose for which You have created me.

☐ With the *Hand of God*, I put my gratitude and thankfulness in their proper perspective and under the Blood of Jesus, *As It Pleases You*. As I look toward Heaven from whence my strength cometh, lead the way, detaching me from any crumb snatchers. Those who seek to take away the BLESSINGS and opportunities that You have graciously provided for me, I rebuke them in the Name of Jesus, redirecting them to carry their own load. For I am grateful for everything in my life, giving You all the GLORY.

☐ With the *Hand of God*, I put my self-discipline, self-mirroring, and self-control in their proper perspective and under the Blood of Jesus, *As It Pleases You*.

Hand-to-Finger Prayer

- ☐ With the *Hand of God*, I put my boundaries and priorities in their proper perspective and under the Blood of Jesus, *As It Pleases You*. I pray for the wisdom to discern the individuals and the situations that have the potential to violate my boundaries in the Name of Jesus. More importantly, please give me the Divine Clarity to recognize their intentions and the discernment to navigate away from their negative influences without blowing my cover or blowing a gasket. While simultaneously exhibiting reliance on the Heavenly of Heavens, according to Your Divine Will and Ways from the Ancient of Days.

- ☐ With the *Hand of God*, I put my communication and conflict resolution skills in their proper perspective and under the Blood of Jesus, *As It Pleases You*. All in all, I need Supernatural Self-Control to take the lessons from my Spiritual Classroom and turn them into MASTERPIECES, feeding Your sheep.

- ☐ With the *Hand of God*, I put my attitude, character, and perception in their proper perspective and under the Blood of Jesus, *As It Pleases You*.

- ☐ With the *Hand of God*, I put my Blueprinted Purpose and Calling in their proper perspective and under the Blood of Jesus, *As It Pleases You*. Father, my God, I know that You will shield me from all hurt, harm, and danger. With the invocation of the Holy Spirit, You will never lead me where I am NOT meant to be. Above all, I completely understand that what belongs to me will be. And what does not belong to me CANNOT remain in the Name of Jesus. So, I will not be swayed by the actions, thoughts, words, or beliefs of crumb snatchers

Hand-to-Finger Prayer

or dream killers. I will continue to move forward in the Spirit of Excellence, pursuing what You have PREDESTINED for me.

☐ With the *Hand of God*, I put my giving back to the Kingdom and Servanthood Charity in their proper perspective and under the Blood of Jesus, *As It Pleases You.*

☐ With the *Hand of God*, I put my stress management and astuteness in their proper perspective and under the Blood of Jesus, *As It Pleases You.*

☐ With the *Hand of God*, I put my setting and achieving goals in their proper perspective and under the Blood of Jesus, *As It Pleases You.*

☐ With the *Hand of God*, I put my sense of belonging in its proper perspective and under the Blood of Jesus, *As It Pleases You.*

☐ With the *Hand of God*, I put overcoming and avoiding bad habits in their proper perspective and under the Blood of Jesus, *As It Pleases You.*

☐ With the *Hand of God*, I put the lust of the eyes, the lusts of the flesh, and the pride of life in their proper perspective and under the Blood of Jesus, *As It Pleases You,* to avoid idolatrous and unhealthy bouts with power, money, sex, status, and fame.

☐ With the *Hand of God*, I put my desires for knowledge, understanding, and power into their proper

Hand-to-Finger Prayer

perspective and under the Blood of Jesus, *As It Pleases You.*

☐ With the *Hand of God*, I put all of my secrets, mysterious pangs of hunger, and idiosyncrasies into their proper perspective and under the Blood of Jesus, *As It Pleases You.*

☐ With the *Hand of God*, I am shifting my perspectives, putting them under the Blood of Jesus, *As It Pleases You.* By Divine Authority, I am DEHORNING the negative plots of the enemy, dismantling their plans with the Blood of Jesus. As You exalt me for being about Your Heavenly Business, *As It Pleases You,* I take possession of my Divine Birthrights, Promises, and Blueprints with no shame attached and with a Divine Trumpet from the Kingdom.

☐ With the *Hand of God*, I thoroughly cover the DOORPOST of my perspectives with the Blood of Jesus as the Holy Spirit guides me into Divine Righteousness, *As It Pleases You.*

☐ With the *Hand of God*, I bring down any form of high-level debauchery. I break it in the Name of Jesus, and I reverse the transaction with the Blood of the Lamb over the DOORPOST of my Mind, Body, Soul, Spirit, Life, Family, and Predestined Blueprint. Please help me to understand that their actions are a reflection of their own struggles, traumas, and insecurities. Thus, with Spiritual Etiquette from the Most High, and *As It Pleases You,* grant me the ability to respond with compassion and grace with the Fruits of the Spirit and Christlike Character.

Hand-to-Finger Prayer

- [ ] With the *Hand of God*, I put my *Hand-to-Finger Approach* into its proper perspective and under the Blood of Jesus, *As It Pleases You*, turning the TABLES in my FAVOR when the timing is right.

From this day forward, with the Blood of the Lamb, I will use the Power of Your Divine Finger toward Your Divine Touch, Restoration, Finetuning, or Regrafting of my character, fruits, thoughts, traumas, conditioning, and beliefs. According to Luke 11:20, "*I with the Finger of God cast out devils, no doubt the kingdom of God has come upon you.*" So on this day:

- [ ] With the *Finger of God*, touch my health with wholeness, wealth, and healing with the Holy Ghost's Fire and Flaming Sword protecting my well-being, Mentally, Physically, Emotionally, and Spiritually, *As It Pleases You* and for Your Divine Glory.

- [ ] With the *Finger of God*, touch my relationships with the Fruits of the Spirit as I become excellent in behaving Christlike, *As It Pleases You* with the Holy Spirit's Blaze of Divine Anointing, clearing my Spiritual Pathway for TAKEOFF and LANDING.

- [ ] With the *Finger of God*, touch my career and my Spiritual Gifts, Purposeful Passion, and Divine Blueprint with the Sacred Flames of the Spirit, igniting the INTERNAL LIGHT from within myself and others, *As It Pleases You*.

Hand-to-Finger Prayer

- ☐ With the *Finger of God*, touch my financial situation, opening up my Spiritual Reservoirs, Divine Provisions, and the Heavenly Negev with the Holy Ghost Fire protecting them, *As It Pleases You*, with good stewardship from the Heavenly of Heavens.

- ☐ With the *Finger of God*, touch my mental and emotional well-being to overcome known and unknown Spiritual Challenges, Quirks, or Traumas as I become a work-in-progress, *As It Pleases You*. Meanwhile, allowing the Power of the Holy Spirit to train me through it, them, or that, cutting to the chase or through the cracks to build a solid foundation.

- ☐ With the *Finger of God*, touch my ability to Spiritually Contend amid internal, earthly, and Spiritual Warfare in the Spirit of Righteousness, Power, and Authority as the Spirit of Holiness remains on high alert, *As It Pleases You*.

- ☐ With the *Finger of God*, touch my Spiritual Growth and Tilling Process with the Sanctified Burst of Fire from the Heavenly of Heavens.

- ☐ With the *Finger of God*, touch my Divine Creativity and Anointed Inspiration with the Fiery Spirit of Holiness, covering and distributing them, *As It Pleases You*.

- ☐ With the *Finger of God*, touch my personal development with the Holy Spirit's Inferno of Divine Greatness.

- ☐ With the *Finger of God*, touch my ability to help others with the Holy Flame of the Spirit proactively going

Hand-to-Finger Prayer

before me, vetting the needs, desires, and wants that must be met, *As It Pleases You.*

☐ With the *Finger of God*, touch my sense of Divine Purpose with the Sanctified Spirit Fire from the Heavenlies.

☐ With the *Finger of God*, touch my communication and people skills with the Divine Blaze of Love, *As It Pleases You.*

☐ With the *Finger of God*, touch my problem-solving abilities with the Holy Spirit's Flaming Power of Articulation and Calculation, penetrating the psyche of mankind, *As It Pleases You.*

☐ With the *Finger of God*, touch my resilience and strength from the Fiery Holy Spirit as I become on fire for the Kingdom of God.

☐ With the *Finger of God*, touch my capacity for love and compassion as the Sacred Flame of the Holy Ghost illuminates my path.

☐ With the *Finger of God*, touch my learning and growth opportunities and capacity as the Holy Spirit's Firestorm of Excellence comes forth as pure gold, *As It Pleases You.*

☐ With the *Finger of God*, touch my bravery and determination with the Flame of Sanctity going before me, *As It Pleases You.*

Hand-to-Finger Prayer

☐ With the *Finger of God*, touch my ability to find joy and fulfillment with the Blaze of Holiness, unveiling the veiled, *As It Pleases You.*

☐ With the *Finger of God*, touch my impact on the world around me with the Flicker of Sacredness that cannot be denied, *As It Pleases You.*

☐ With the *Finger of God*, touch my ability to make a positive difference with an undeniable Spark of Blessedness.

☐ With the *Finger of God*, touch my overall happiness and peace of mind, posing a Flare of Purity unlike no other, *As It Pleases You.*

☐ With the *Finger of God*, touch my reconciling abilities with a Spiritual Blanket of Holiness and Righteousness, *As It Pleases You.*

☐ With the *Finger of God*, touch my courage and determination with a Spiritual Roar that can be heard in the Heavenlies, *As It Pleases You.*

☐ With the *Finger of God*, I release all guilt, shame, anxiety, fear, and confusion with a Sanctified Burst of Faith, *As It Pleases You.*

☐ With the *Finger of God*, I detach myself from all soul ties, yokes, or bondages as the Fiery Spirit of Holiness severs them, *As It Pleases You.*

Hand-to-Finger Prayer

- ☐ With the *Finger of God*, I cut the cords of all ungodly entanglements as the Fiery Holy Spirit creates a Divine Smokescreen to deliver me, *As It Pleases You*.

- ☐ With the *Finger of God*, I reverse-engineer anything hindering my Divine Blueprinted Purpose from coming forth with the Holy Spirit Inferno cued up at all times to protect me and it, *As It Pleases You*.

- ☐ With the *Finger of God*, cleanse my Mind, Body, Soul, and Spirit from all ungodly contaminants as the Sacred Fire of the Holy Spirit purifies me in real-time. I confess my sins, repenting of them all and seeking Divine Forgiveness, *As It Pleases You*.

- ☐ With the *Finger of God*, I usher in peace, prosperity, and oneness in my life as the Firestorm of the Holy Spirit brings forth Divine Revelation, *As It Pleases You*.

- ☐ With the *Finger of God*, I give thanks in all things as my tongue becomes the pen of a ready writer with the Holy Spirit's Inferno from the Heavenly of Heavens guiding me in my Heaven on Earth Experiences.

If I, by the Finger of God with the Holy Seal of Grace, hereby command with the unction of the Holy Spirit to ___(state the specific request or action)___ , in the Name of Jesus. By the Authority Vested in me, I declare and decree the Hand of God over ___(state the general request or action)___ .

In my *Hand-to-Finger Approach*, from this day forward, I place a Spiritual Seal on my Heaven on Earth Experiences, *As It Pleases You*, with all of my hope, faith, and trust, in You, my Heavenly Father, Amen.

Throne Room 8

Heavenly Throne Room Prayer

The Throne, the Throne, the Throne of the Most High God, I commit my life to You. In the Name of Jesus, You have given me this Sacred Space that is ordained for Your Divine Glory. As I dedicate this Sacred Space to You with sprinkles of GOLD, fill it now with Your Holy Presence and Spiritual Absolutes.

I surrender to the Holy Trinity, becoming ONE. Thus, remove all ungodly desecrations, declarations, and demarcations as I apply the Blood of Jesus to the DOORPOST of my Mind, Body, Soul, and Spirit. I am also anointing the DOORPOST of this Sacred Space, protecting me and my family from the works, distractions, and tricks of the enemy with a LEGION of watching and warring Angels on full alert 24/7.

My enemies will not be able to pinpoint or track my next move due to the Spiritual Covering of the Blood of Jesus on the DOORPOST of my life. By Divine Authority and the Cycles of Life, those who violate my free will or boundaries will turn on themselves and fall by their own counsel based on the Spiritual Law of Seedtime and Harvest.

With all of the Spiritual Power vested in me, I repent of all of my atrocities that may give my enemies an open door, an open invitation, or a reason to set false expectations. So, I close the door right now in the Name of Jesus, terminating and

Heavenly Throne Room Prayer

overturning every legality, oversight, and technicality on my behalf.

In this Heavenly Throne Room, I overturn every Spirit of Sickness, Spirit of Setback, Buckling Spirit, or Spirit of Stubbornness. They must expire right now, in the Name of Jesus, as I usher in the Spirit of Greatness to incorporate the following, but NOT limited to such:

- ☐ In this Heavenly Throne Room, I usher in the Spirit of Wholeness and Health.
- ☐ In this Heavenly Throne Room, I introduce the Spirit of Prosperity and Proactiveness.
- ☐ In this Heavenly Throne Room, I initiate the Spirit of Attainment and Astuteness.
- ☐ In this Heavenly Throne Room, I commence the Spirit of Progress and Preparedness.
- ☐ In this Heavenly Throne Room, I set in motion the Spirit of Advancement and Achievement.
- ☐ In this Heavenly Throne Room, I mark the commencement of the Spirit of Success and Sanctity.
- ☐ In this Heavenly Throne Room, I usher in the Spirit of Triumph and Tenacity.
- ☐ In this Heavenly Throne Room, I introduce the Spirit of Victory and Virtue.
- ☐ In this Heavenly Throne Room, I initiate the Spirit of Improvement and Integrity.
- ☐ In this Heavenly Throne Room, I commence the Spirit of Betterment and Bodaciousness.
- ☐ In this Heavenly Throne Room, I set in motion the Spirit of Development and Discipline.
- ☐ In this Heavenly Throne Room, I spark the Spirit of Growth and Grandeur.
- ☐ In this Heavenly Throne Room, I invoke the Spirit of Self-Control, Self-Mirroring, and Self-Analysis.

Heavenly Throne Room Prayer

- [ ] In this Heavenly Throne Room, I bring forth the Spirit of Eloquence, Savvy, Organization, and Perfect Timing.

My Lord, as Your Divine Shield and Favor encompass me, I come into the unwavering Presence of my Wonderful Counselor. As I come before You today with gratefulness and the correct heart posture, in the Name of Jesus, I seek Your Divine Wisdom, Understanding, Strength, and Guidance.

In this Throne Room, *Spirit to Spirit*, I step beyond the natural realm into the Supernatural, *As It Pleases You*. As You cover me with Your Spiritual Veil in my Throne Room:

- [ ] Remove the scales from my eyes so that I can see beyond the physical into the Spiritual Realm with Divine Accuracy and Precision, *As It Pleases You*.

- [ ] Open my ears to hear beyond the physical into the Spiritual Realm with Divine Accuracy, Precision, and Discernment, *As It Pleases You*.

- [ ] Open my mouth to speak into the Spiritual Realm with my Spiritual Tongue or Words flowing in perfect harmony with Your Divine Language and Utterances from the Holy Spirit, *As It Pleases You*.

In my Throne Room with the Holy of Holies, I seek Divine Deliverance from the inside out, purging my human nature for a Godly one to connect to You, *Spirit to Spirit*. Father, I surrender the depths of my soul to You, getting rid of impatience, insecurity, insufficiency, unpredictability, idolatry, instability, irrationality, vulnerability, and all forms of immorality unpleasing to You. By the Blood of the Lamb, with the assistance of the Holy Spirit, usher in patience,

Heavenly Throne Room Prayer

security, sufficiency, stability, humility, consistency, rationality, and morality.

In Your Divine Presence, O Lord, I will not be at a loss for words in our *Spirit to Spirit* Communion as my tongue becomes the pen of a ready writer while the Holy Spirit makes intercession for me. Therefore, I renounce all deep-rooted problems associated with all of my known and unknown debaucherous efforts, uncontrolled thoughts, perversions, violence, lies, chaos, confusion, bad habits, hopelessness, hatefulness, rudeness, despair, anger, shame, materialism, guilt, and nervousness. I demand their exit out of this Throne Room right now, in the Name of Jesus.

I replace these negative characteristics with self-control, disciplined thoughts of positivity, purity, peace, order, clarity, good habits, hope, joy, love, contentment, confidence, astuteness, rationale, truthfulness, authenticity, and calmness in the Name of Jesus. As I speak these positive attributes into the atmosphere, I Spiritually Seal them with the Blood of Jesus on the DOORPOST of my Mind, Body, Soul, and Spirit.

Lord, I reclaim my Spiritual Rights, Power, and Territory as I lay claim to all of my BLESSINGS and BLUEPRINT. Father, in the Name of Jesus, You have given me power over the adversary, so I release myself and my family from anything or anyone holding us back from PLEASING You.

I cancel any curse, bondage, yoke, or soul tie blocking or hindering me. Thus, I invoke the Holy Spirit to cover my Mind, Body, Soul, and Spirit with the Blood of Jesus, bringing me into Your Sacred Space of Holiness and Purity in or out of The Throne Room, *As It Pleases You.*

Thank you for being my Divine Source of strength and for always being there to guide me in Spirit and Truth. In Jesus' Name, I pray, in humility and sincerity with joy and praise, Amen.

Throne Room 9

Holy Communion Prayer

My Omnipotent Father of all, I humbly gather in Your Divine Presence, *Spirit to Spirit*, for Holy Communion. Thank you for the opportunity to remember the SACRIFICE of Your Son, Jesus Christ, and to renew my faith and commitment to You. As I take this bread and drink this cup, I do so with reverence and gratitude in the Sacred Act of Divine Connection, *Spirit to Spirit*.

By the Blood of the Lamb, I recommit myself to living in unity with fellow Believers and in obedience to the Word of God. As I become Spiritually Sensitive to Your Divine Will and Ways, with the power vested in me, I break down all walls erected that are unpleasing to You, my Heavenly Father. I relinquish every ungodly power over me, breaking every yoke stifling my Holy Communion with You.

- ☐ In my *Spirit to Spirit* Session of Holy Communion with You, I sever ties with the Spirit of Oppression, replacing it with the Spirit of Empowerment, Dignity, and Resilience, *As It Pleases You*.

- ☐ In my *Spirit to Spirit* Session of Holy Communion with You, I break the bonds of having a slavery mentality, replacing it with a free will mentality, *As It Pleases You*.

Holy Communion Prayer

☐ In my *Spirit to Spirit* Session of Holy Communion with You, I terminate the chains of having a scarcity mentality, replacing it with a More-Than-Enough and the Lord-Will-Provide Mindset, *As It Pleases You.*

☐ In my *Spirit to Spirit* Session of Holy Communion with You, I end the negative mental chatter, replacing it with positive mental chatter and goodwill, *As It Pleases You.*

☐ In my *Spirit to Spirit* Session of Holy Communion with You, I bring to an end the Spirit of Non-Productivity, replacing it with the Spirit of Productivity and Spiritually Tilling my own ground, *As It Pleases You.*

☐ In my *Spirit to Spirit* Session of Holy Communion with You, I bring a halt to the Spirit of Deception, replacing it with the Spirit of Honesty, Fairness, and Justice, *As It Pleases You.*

☐ In my *Spirit to Spirit* Session of Holy Communion with You, I depart from the Spirit of Mockery, replacing it with the Spirit of Respect, Humility, Esteem, and Relatability, *As It Pleases You.*

☐ In my *Spirit to Spirit* Session of Holy Communion with You, I cut the cord to the Spirit of Confusion, replacing it with the Spirit of Peace, Unity, and Understanding, *As It Pleases You.*

☐ In my *Spirit to Spirit* Session of Holy Communion with You, I cancel the Spirit of Frustration, replacing it with the Spirit of Calmness, Patience, and Persistence, *As It Pleases You.*

Holy Communion Prayer

- ☐ In my *Spirit to Spirit* Session of Holy Communion with You, I terminate the Spirit of Forgetfulness, replacing it with the Spirit of Remembrance, Recognition, and Relevance, *As It Pleases You.*

- ☐ In my *Spirit to Spirit* Session of Holy Communion with You, I cast down the Spirit of Slothfulness, replacing it with the Spirit of Diligence, Direction, and Determination, *As It Pleases You.*

- ☐ In my *Spirit to Spirit* Session of Holy Communion with You, I renounce all ungodly roadblocks, replacing them with the Spirit of Divine Direction, Illumination, and Guidance, *As It Pleases You.*

- ☐ In my *Spirit to Spirit* Session of Holy Communion with You, I rebuke the Spirit of Anger, replacing it with the Spirit of Peace, Calmness, and Love, *As It Pleases You.*

- ☐ In my *Spirit to Spirit* Session of Holy Communion with You, I break the yoke of the Spirit of Distraction, replacing it with the Spirit of Focus, Concentration, and Single-Mindedness, *As It Pleases You.*

My Father, I understand that Holiness is what You desire from me...Holiness is who You are...Holiness is PLEASING to You...Holiness is what You do...Holiness is what I do, in the Name of Jesus. In the Spirit of Holiness, here is what I bring to the Throne Room in the Name of Jesus:

- ☐ In Holiness, *As It Pleases You,* I confess all my sins before You. Bring back my soul from the Pit that You may be

Holy Communion Prayer

enlightened with the Light of Life. I humbly repent of them and ask for Your forgiveness, and I cast down the Spirit of Disobedience to bring forth Divine Obedience in the Spirit of Excellence.

- ☐ In Holiness, *As It Pleases You*, I give thanks for my common sense to bring forth the Spirit of Wisdom with Divine Secrets and Treasures from the Heavenly of Heavens.

- ☐ In Holiness, *As It Pleases You*, I cancel the Spirit of Disobedience, ushering in Divine Respectfulness and Humility from the Ancient of Days to my present actionable efforts. Father, You have delivered my soul from death and kept my feet from falling so that I may walk before You in the light of the living. Thus, obedience to You is my reasonable service.

- ☐ In Holiness, *As It Pleases You*, I put away a lying or loose tongue, bringing forth word and mouth control, setting a Spiritual Guard over my mouth. Father, once I open my mouth, allow my words and Spiritual Language to become smooth as butter and sweet as honey, tantalizing the hearts and minds of those I come in contact with.

- ☐ In Holiness, *As It Pleases You*, I forgive all acts of betrayal or treachery on my behalf or that of another. With a contrite and repenting heart, I bring forth the Spirit of Loyalty and Faithfulness to reconcile my heart posture from worldly to Kingdom with the Fruits of the Spirit and Christlike Character.

- ☐ In Holiness, *As It Pleases You*, I bring a complete halt to any Spirit of Oppression, the Spirit of Weakness, and

Holy Communion Prayer

the Spirit of Helplessness. By the Blood of Jesus, I invoke the Spirit of Freedom, Strength, Power, Empowerment, and Interdependence.

☐ In Holiness, *As It Pleases You*, I cast down the Spirit of Dead works, bringing forth the Spirit of Progressiveness, Proactiveness, Productivity, and Preparedness while Spiritually Tilling my own ground to GROW better, stronger, and wiser.

☐ In Holiness, *As It Pleases You*, I ask that anything stolen from me be RESTORED 100-fold, in the Name of Jesus. I declare and decree that Divine Restoration and Restitution of what was lost must be returned to me with interest. For Divine Justice is in full effect as the Fire of the Holy Ghost fills my life with Divine Abundance, Overflow, and Blessings. I trust in Your Infinite Wisdom and Love, making all things possible.

☐ In Holiness, *As It Pleases You*, I cancel all word curses over my life, reversing all negative words to positive words without becoming accident-prone or clumsy, in the Name of Jesus. I rebuke this feebleness, allowing the Holy Spirit to set a Spiritual Guide, Cover, and Guard over my life, strengthening my loins from the inside out. From this day forward, I speak positively, creating wins and becoming grateful for all things.

☐ In Holiness, *As It Pleases You*, I give up and relinquish all my rebellion to embrace the Spirit of Tenacity, Oneness, and Unity as I submit myself to Your Divine Will and Ways.

☐ In Holiness, *As It Pleases You*, I forgive all who have harmed me, wronged me, or thrown me under the bus

Holy Communion Prayer

as I release all forms of soul bondage in the Name of Jesus. As I invoke the Divine Presence of the Holy Spirit, I no longer participate in destructive or abnormal patterns or habits for self-pleasure. I usher in the Spirit of Selflessness, being about my Heavenly Father's Business in Earthen Vessel.

- ☐ In Holiness, *As It Pleases You*, I commit myself to serve and obey You, remaining in good standing in the Kingdom, reclaiming my Spiritual Ground to my Tree of Life. In Jesus' worthy name for my Heaven on Earth Experience, I am no longer problematic. I am a bona fide problem-solver for the Kingdom, doing what I have been called to do, leaving no stone unturned and no willing man behind in the Spirit of Oneness.

- ☐ In Holiness, *As It Pleases You*, Lord, I take my stand against and renounce every dark and evil force, negative trigger, or unresolved trauma that has entered my life, rendering them powerless, in the Name of Jesus. Under the Divine Blood, I replace them with the Spirit of Illumination, Light, Goodness, Wholeness, and Healing.

- ☐ In Holiness, *As It Pleases You*, and in Your GOOD PLEASURE, I shake myself loose from control, manipulation, domination, and bullying. At the same time, canceling all forms of lying, cheating, stealing, gossiping, criticizing, envy, jealousy, pride, coveting, and the competitiveness associated with them. In the Mighty Name of Jesus, I reverse all of these negative characteristics with a Spiritual Compass upholding truthfulness, honesty, ethics, trustworthiness, praise, contentment, trust, humility, contentedness, and teamwork.

Holy Communion Prayer

☐ In Holiness, *As It Pleases You,* I surrender to the Gifts of the Holy Spirit to bring Divine Glory to the Kingdom. As the Holy Spirit operates through me, I give way to total humility and become the Crème de la Crème of the Kingdom of Heaven.

☐ In Holiness, *As It Pleases You*, I cast down any form of sexual, physical, mental, verbal, or emotional abuse or enslavement. More importantly, I silence all Spiritual Abuse inflicted upon me or my family in the Name of Jesus. I usher in the Spirit of Servanthood and Good Will from the Kingdom of God.

With many BLESSINGS from the Heavens Above with Divine Unity, Harmony, and Mercy, in the Name of Jesus, I pray. Amen.

Throne Room 10

Stepping Stones Prayer

My Eternal, Loving, and Merciful Father, I come to You in the Name of Jesus, surrendering every *Stepping Stone* of my past, present, and future to You. Help me see that every step I take leads to Your Divine Glory and my Predestined Blueprinted training, testing, and positioning.

Each *Stepping Stone* that I step on is placed for a purpose, and even when my path is rocky, I know that You are there to support and guide me. For this reason, I proactively THANK YOU as I walk by faith and not by sight, in the Name of Jesus.

In every *Stepping Stone*, there are actions, thoughts, and choices involved; thus, I am respectfully laying the breaded stones of MANNA on the Spiritual Table of Showbread. In this Throne Room, the Divine Provisions are made evident for the Spiritual Covenant between You, my Heavenly Father, and I, the Servant of the Kingdom.

On this Table of Presence, *As It Pleases You*, the Sacredness of Your Divine Alliance is established and SEALED in the Heavenly of Heavens. This Symbolic Reminder represents the constant and selfless *Spirit to Spirit* Fellowship that You desire from me.

Father, as I cover my *Stepping Stones*, one by one, they will represent the Spiritual Food needed to nourish my Mind, Body, Soul, and Spirit, *As It Pleases You* to bring forth unity and wholeness to all mankind.

Stepping Stones Prayer

When properly discerning my *Stepping Stones* and being about my Father's Business, *As It Pleases You*, help me to avoid unequally yoked people, places, and things unpleasing to You, unless it is a part of my Spiritual Classroom of training, testing, calibrating, and processing. With this enduring and unbreakable connection between me and my faith in the Holy Trinity, I invoke the Divine Love and Presence of the Holy of Holies to come forth in the Name of Jesus.

In this Throne Room, *As It Pleases You*, and as a Servant of the Kingdom of Heaven, envelop me with the comfort, guidance, strength, and astuteness needed to move forward in the Spirit of Excellence, leaving no stone unturned and no WILLING vessel behind.

- ☐ When properly discerning my Stepping Stones, *As It Pleases You*, and as I consider my Spiritual Path, please guide me to follow it with integrity and without hypocrisy, according to Your Divine Will, while helping me to avoid living by a double standard unpleasing to You.

- ☐ When I carefully consider my Stepping Stones, *As It Pleases You*, and as I carefully contemplate my Spiritual Journey, please assist me in living by example. Thus, if I am unwanted and rejected, grant me the Divine Courage to shake the dust off my feet with my head held high while moving forward in the Spirit of Excellence.

- ☐ When I carefully consider my Stepping Stones, *As It Pleases You*, and in reflecting on my Spiritual Endeavors, please lend me a hand in pinpointing or overcoming victimization plots. My God, grant me the ability to extract the lessons, wisdom, and understanding to feed Your sheep for a time such as this.

Stepping Stones Prayer

- ☐ When I carefully consider my Stepping Stones, *As It Pleases You*, and as I ponder over my Spiritual Course, please aid me in getting rid of selfishness and pridefulness. Instead, I invoke the Fruits of the Spirit, becoming Christlike and exhibiting the humility and selflessness needed to perfect my people skills.

- ☐ When I carefully consider my Stepping Stones, *As It Pleases You*, and as I consider my Spiritual Progression, please have my back on getting rid of every bit of hatefulness within my loins. Today, I invoke the Spirit of Pleasantness, allowing it to permeate my every step without having to degrade or put down anyone. With the presence of the Holy Spirit, I build, inspire, encourage, and motivate in the Name of Jesus.

- ☐ When I carefully consider my Stepping Stones, *As It Pleases You*, and as I contemplate my Spiritual Development, please assist me with not violating my conscience. Lord, grant me the Spiritual Sensitivity needed to DISCERN the nudging of the Holy Spirit, red flags, rotten fruits, distractions, and wolves in sheep's clothing.

- ☐ When I carefully consider my Stepping Stones, *As It Pleases You*, and as I deliberate over my Spiritual Passage, please give me a boost when people attempt to drag me through the dirt or mud. Lord, clean me up and wash me white a snow, purifying my Mind, Body, Soul, and Spirit on a moment-by-moment basis.

- ☐ When I carefully consider my Stepping Stones, *As It Pleases You*, and as I navigate my Spiritual Channel, please extend added favor in helping me to exhibit self-

Stepping Stones Prayer

control, self-analysis, self-mirroring, and self-correcting.

☐ When I carefully consider my Stepping Stones, *As It Pleases You*, and as I focus on my Spiritual Course, please guide me on how to be my authentic self, doing what I have been called to do. Father, I understand that You did not make a mistake when You created me. So, I stand firmly on Your Divine Choice about me and heed the Heavenly Call in confidence without tiptoeing around it, them, or that, in the Name of Jesus.

☐ When I carefully consider my Stepping Stones, *As It Pleases You*, and as I explore my Spiritual Apparatus, please stand by me as I contend with the dualism. Father, I request Divine Guidance in converting negatives to positives, wrong to right, unjust to just, unrighteousness to righteous, hate to love, darkness to light, and so on.

☐ When I carefully consider my Stepping Stones, *As It Pleases You*, and as I calibrate my Spiritual Compass, please support me in casting down the Pharisee's Spirit, combating any hypocritical tendencies and hidden insecurities leading to any form of jealousy, envy, pride, greed, coveting, or competitiveness. For this reason, I usher in the Spirit of Authenticity and Relevance in the Name of Jesus and in the Spirit of Truth. By the Blood of the Lamb, I reverse negative characteristics into secure, positive, soft people skills to incorporate openness, unity, contentment, humility, generosity, gratefulness, helpfulness, and cooperation.

☐ When I carefully consider my Stepping Stones, *As It Pleases You*, and as I implore my Spiritual Team of

Stepping Stones Prayer

Oneness, I kindly seek restoration and healing of any anger problems, hidden or unresolved traumas, or negative mental chattering causing me to relive my past. Today, on this Divine Throne, I lay to rest all of my known and unknown negative triggers, insensitivities, rudeness, or condescending behaviors. Contrarily, I invoke positive triggers, attentiveness, respectfulness, selflessness, kindness, and impartiality in the Name of Jesus.

☐ When I carefully consider my Stepping Stones, *As It Pleases You*, and as I think with a Kingdomly Mindset, please encourage me to become patient when in my Spiritual Classroom, Spiritual Training, Spiritual Testing, or Spiritual Tilling Phases amid any frustration and provocations of impatience. Father, in the Name of Jesus, grant me the strength, wisdom, and know-how to cultivate patience in my Mind, Body, Soul, and Spirit from the Heavens Above. I understand that everything happens in its own time, so Lord, grant me the ability and insight to wait with grace, gratefulness, resilience, and composure with the wisdom to know when to speak and when to listen. When to hold and when to fold. When to do and when not to do. When to resolve and when to dissolve. When to engage and when to disengage in the Name of Jesus.

☐ When I carefully consider my Stepping Stones, *As It Pleases You*, and as a Servant of the Kingdom, I squash the Spirit of Confrontation. Father, my God, in the Name of Jesus, I am seeking guidance and strength from You on how to approach difficult situations with a Spirit of Understanding and Empathy rather than becoming defensive or aggressive. In this Throne

Stepping Stones Prayer

Room with the Power of the Holy Spirit, I RISE above it all.

☐ When I carefully consider my Stepping Stones, *As It Pleases You*, and as I journey toward Spiritual Growth of Learning and Grooming from the Heavenly of Heavens, I come before You today, my Father. In the Name of Jesus, I invoke an instrument of harmony, discretion, and reconciliation. I am open and receptive to Your Divine Will, Wisdom, Nurturing, and Positioning. Thus, I surrender to having a Teachable and Humble Spirit as I deepen my *Spirit to Spirit* Relations with You.

☐ When I carefully consider my Stepping Stones, *As It Pleases You*, and as I venture toward Spiritual Maturity, I release the better and greater version of who You designed me to be. With strength and perseverance, Spiritually Groom me in the ways You see fit with love, kindness, mercy, and compassion. My God, I am open to You...I will not compromise, nor will I leave any stone unturned or uncharted. By Divine Decree, I will extract the hidden wisdom under each stone to contribute to my Cornerstone of Greatness.

☐ When I carefully consider my Stepping Stones, *As It Pleases You*, and as I pursue Spiritual Enlightenment, I unleash my Spiritual Discerning Faculties befitting for the Kingdom. In Your HOLINESS, bring light to my areas of darkness, exposing them to the Holy of Holies, excommunicating all of the doubt, disbelief, distrust, conflict, and distractions in the Name of Jesus. From this point forward, I interject trust, confidence, faith, belief, consistency, and alignment with the Holy Ghost Fire of Divine Elevation with a River of Provisional Life.

Stepping Stones Prayer

☐ When I carefully consider my Stepping Stones, *As It Pleases You*, and as I invoke Spiritual Illumination, I will lift Your Divine Name on HIGH. Father, my God, in the Name of Jesus, as I put on my Royal Robe of Greatness, I invoke the Holy Spirit with the Spiritual Seals from the Throne of God to bring forth the Divine Light needed to illuminate my Spiritual Path. All of this allows me to see clearly, and make decisions that are aligned with Your Divine Will as You keep me in perfect peace with my mind stayed on You. Moreover, while in a state of conscious peace, I willfully add You into the equation of all things, regardless of its difficulty or simplicity. In my steadfastness, O Lord, open my Spiritual Eyes, Ears, and Language to Divine Insights and Revelations that bring light to those around me, in the Name of Jesus.

☐ When I carefully consider my Stepping Stones, *As It Pleases You*, and as I usher in Spiritual Understanding from the Heavenly Host from the Kingdom of God with the whispers of Divine Authority, hear me, O Lord. My Heavenly Creator, bring forth my effectiveness and creativity in Earthen Vessel and for my Heaven on Earth Experience. As I Spiritually Till my own ground, I reject anyone placing my Mind, Body, Soul, and Spirit in a box, in the Name of Jesus. I reject becoming boxed or blocked by the enemy's wiles. From this point onward, from the Throne Room of the Most High God, I will think inside, outside, over, under, around, and through the box, extracting every lesson, experience, or quality needed to go to the next level, breaking the limits of mediocrity.

☐ When I carefully consider my Stepping Stones, *As It Pleases You*, and as I contemplate Spiritual

Stepping Stones Prayer

Amplification, I remove all ungodly ulterior motives from my repertoire. Father, I expose my heart posture to You, breaking all forms of hexing, vexing, negative indexing, or doxing designed to bring shame to my name or make a liar out of You. As the Bride of Christ, in the same way as Your Divine Grace and Mercy that You covered Adam and Eve. I, too, cannot sew leaves together to cover myself; therefore, I invoke my personalized Spiritual Garment to COVER me and my nakedness. It is my Divine Birthright, so I claim it right now in the Name of Jesus. Thus, no weapon formed against me shall prosper because the Blood of Jesus covers me. In the Spirit of Oneness, *As It Pleases You*, every tongue that negatively or unjustly rises against me shall be condemned by the Holy of Holies while becoming a Stepping Stone for my Divine Cornerstone.

- ☐ When I carefully consider my Stepping Stones, *As It Pleases You*, and in my quest for Spiritual Unity, I appreciate You, and I am committed to the Mission of the Kingdom. I will not become lukewarm, dull, stiff-necked, or straddle the fence; I am all in...in the Name of Jesus. Nor will I become sidetracked by the issues of life. In this Throne Room, I am ten-toes deep in my Blueprinted Mission. As I stand before You today in a unified effort, please help me stay true to my Divine Purpose, granting me the perseverance needed to overcome any obstacles that may come my way.

- ☐ When I carefully consider my Stepping Stones, *As It Pleases You*, and for my Heaven on Earth Experience, when I fall short, help me to know Your Divine Ways. O Lord, as You teach me, show me, nudge me, and test me on the Spiritual Paths toward evolving into my highest and best use, make every Stepping Stone a

Stepping Stones Prayer

potential FOOTSTOOL for my Divine Cornerstone, in the Name of Jesus.

- ☐ When I carefully consider my Stepping Stones, *As It Pleases You*, and in Earthen Vessel, please make my path straight, as I walk in it as You establish my steps.

- ☐ When I carefully consider my Stepping Stones, *As It Pleases You*, let any Spirit of Poverty or Lack be overturned in the Name of Jesus. I pray for Divine Provisions, and I declare SUPERNATURAL supplies, rations, and increases based on Your Divine Covenantal Blueprint and Promises.

In this Throne Room: *As It Pleases You*, Your word is a LAMP to my feet and a LIGHT to my path, and I TRUST them to do what they are designed to do. My Lord, I acknowledge Your Divine Sovereignty and the immeasurable depth of Your Supernatural Wisdom; therefore, with my *Stepping Stones*, order my steps as only You can do. As I navigate through the twists and turns, clear my path as only You can do.

Above all, when the shadows of despair loom over my life, Divinely Illuminate the way with a Heavenly Cloud by day and a Supernatural Pillar of Smoke by night with Your Divine Power on HIGH. Lord, with a made-up mind, with clarity of thought, along with my strength of focus, *As It Pleases You*, lead me through the uncertain terrain that lies ahead, and allow me to put my past behind me to embrace the PROMISE.

As I lift my prayers to You, my Heavenly Father, surround me with Your peace...A peace that surpasses all understanding. As Your Divine Presence fills the space in my Mind, Body, Soul, and Spirit, please allow our personal *Spirit to Spirit* Relationship to radiate outwardly through every fiber of my being. Let it be a HEALING BALM, offering peace and

Stepping Stones Prayer

solace to those around me without me having to say one word. And Lord, when I do speak, allow my words to encourage and build others in a way that leads them back to the Kingdom, *As It Pleases You.* With reverence, honor, and devotion, in the Name of Jesus, I STEP for You, with You, and through You. Amen.

Throne Room 11

The Cornerstone Prayer

My Creator of all things, my Heavenly Father, my Cornerstone is Your Cornerstone, and Your Cornerstone is mine, for we are ONE in Christ Jesus. In the stillness of this Divine Moment, *Spirit to Spirit*, I come before You, grounded in humility, love, and faith, surrounded by Your Divine Light of MERCY.

My Lord, My Heavenly Father, I acknowledge You as my Cornerstone of Divine Greatness, and I am created in Your Divine Image in an Earthen Vessel for my Heaven on Earth Experiences that You have PREDESTINED. For this reason, O' Lord, I call upon Your Infinite Wisdom to expel any Spiritual Blindness, Deafness, or Muteness that may cloud my sense of good judgment, reasoning, understanding, or hinder my ability to communicate effectively with You, myself, and others.

With a heart full of gratitude, I open my Mind, Body, Soul, and Spirit to the Spiritual Tilling (Cultivation) Process. Based on the Laws of Love and Liberty, for the record, the treasures of my heart are with You, first and foremost. With this willful and conscious decision, my Divine Reverence lies with the Kingdom of God and with whom I serve. I commit myself completely to the Cornerstone of Greatness to maximize my full potential and my reason for being.

In my Heaven on Earth Experiences, I permit the light of God to BLESS me in an infinite number of ways, through an infinite number of channels, to bring to me what I desire,

The Cornerstone Prayer

according to my Predestined Blueprint. I release any blockage that would withhold from me that which I desire and what aligns with my Predestined Blueprint.

Father, my God, as Your Cornerstone, heal me, expand me, feed me, support me, love me, and envelope me with Your Divine Presence, in the Name of Jesus. Above all, develop my *Spirit to Spirit* Relations, Spiritual Etiquette, Christlike Character, and people skills with the Fruits of the Spirit, *As It Pleases You.*

Lord, in this work-in-progress, pruning, or developmental phase, if someone leaves me or walks away when I am a diamond in the rough, please strengthen me to let go with no strings attached, with a smile on my face. Secondly, perfect my response to say, 'God bless you, thank you for the lesson or experience, and goodbye!' Thirdly, help me to end the conversation or draw a line in the sand without violating anyone's free will or holding grudges because my Mind, Body, Soul, or Spirit is NOT the Devil's playground.

As a Cornerstone of Divine Greatness, my MINDSET is locked in on a positive, non-violent, and free-will zone. I do not need to fight for someone who chooses not to be in my life. Nor do I want to remain where I am unwanted, abused, neglected, shunned, rejected, or traumatized. By the Blood of the Lamb, I call this out for what it is; therefore, I am free to usher in adornment, value, acceptance, support, love, and being wanted. Father, grant me the courage to selflessly recognize my worth, to adorn myself with positivity with self-love, and to offer the same acceptance to others, *As It Pleases You.*

As a Cornerstone of Greatness, I pray for wisdom to seek and embrace the support I need in times of difficulty and to become a source of support, inspiration, and a bedrock for those around me. As my Guiding Light, allow love to permeate through my heart, guiding my posture, attitude, words, thoughts, and actions, allowing me to extend

The Cornerstone Prayer

kindness, mercy, and compassion to all I encounter, *As It Pleases You.*

In Your Divine Presence, I must save time and energy to glean the Meat of the Word of God, putting away the milking stages of folly, distractions, and creativity blockers to create an environment WORTHY of Your Divine Presence.

Awaken Holy Spirit, Awaken Holy Spirit, Awaken Holy Spirit, the Servant of God is listening. Speak Lord, Speak Lord, Speak Lord, Your Servant is listening. The Blood, the Blood, the Blood, the Covering of the Blood of Jesus is beckoned, as the FOOTSTOOLS of my enemies must come forth as recompense for wasting my precious time. Pay up, pay up, pay up now, in the Name of Jesus.

My Heavenly Father, the goal of my Divine Cornerstone is to win amid an apparent lose-lose. When opening my Spiritual Eyes to see, I need Your help in the EXTRACTING and CONVERTING process of maintaining a Positive Mental Mindset and allowing my VALUE to become far above RUBIES. By the Blood of the Lamb, I glean the lessons, principles, character traits, instincts, and eloquence associated with speaking, understanding, and relaying Your Divine Language on Your Terms.

Through the power of the HOLY SPIRIT with Divine Illumination, I connect the dots of my life with my Divine Destiny, invoking Divine Revelations from the Heavenly of Heavens.

☐ On this Divine Cornerstone, I connect the dots of preparedness, proactiveness, and awareness, as I no longer play by my own rules. Instead, I play by the Spiritual Rules of the Kingdom with the Word of God in hand. As I abide in You, grant me the Spiritual Alignment required to become disciplined, prepared, and accountable, preventing me from venturing into a Spiritual Violation zone or cursing my own hand. So, I

The Cornerstone Prayer

purge all ungodly or negative chatter blocking the Light of God, the Kingdom, or my ability to be fruitful and multiply.

☐ With my Cornerstone of Divine Greatness, I will be productive in the Name of Jesus with Spiritual Guidance from the Holy of Holies while covering myself with the Blood of Jesus as Spiritual Atonement.

☐ With my Cornerstone of Divine Greatness, I will increase to gain Spiritual Privilege and the Favor of God, as well as with man through Godly Character Traits and the Mind of Christ.

☐ With my Cornerstone of Divine Greatness, I sow, till, and reproduce to bring forth my Inner Genius to overcome, create, and conquer.

☐ With my Cornerstone of Divine Greatness, I will activate the Law of Reciprocity according to the Spiritual Law of Seedtime and Harvest, giving and sharing for the Greater Good.

☐ With my Cornerstone of Divine Greatness, I will overcome, learn, grow, and sow back into the Kingdom.

☐ With my Cornerstone of Divine Greatness, I take full responsibility for my Spiritual Gifts, Divine Blueprint, the Fruits of the Spirit, Christlike Character, and my Heaven on Earth Experiences.

☐ With my Cornerstone of Divine Greatness, I place a Spiritual Demand on gaining access to the Divine

The Cornerstone Prayer

Wisdom, Treasures, and Secrets from the Ancient of Days.

- ☐ With my Cornerstone of Divine Greatness, I set a guard over my Mind, Body, Soul, and Spirit to usher in a Positive Mental Attitude to create a win-win out of everything and with everyone.

- ☐ With my Cornerstone of Divine Greatness, I enforce my Spiritual Rights to Divine Insight by removing Spiritual Blindness, Deafness, or Muteness.

- ☐ With my Cornerstone of Divine Greatness, I exhibit my Divine Rights over any known or unknown battles or traumas of fear, anger, doubt, unbelief, complaining, guilt, worry, shame, resentment, or discontentment. Anything or anyone that is intended to keep me distracted, overwhelmed, or confused, I rebuke it or them in the Name of Jesus. In addition, I proactively reverse engineer any self-imposed battles into courage, calmness, peace, certainty, faith, gratitude, innocence, trust, forgiveness, contentment, and satisfaction.

In this Holy Place, I invoke my Spiritual Rights to Divine Clarity, while heeding my Cornerstone of Divine Greatness. As I become receptive to Your Divine Will and Ways, I also invoke my Divine Rights to hear the Divine Whispers of Your Supernatural Guidance as You speak love and truth, with an unspeakable infusion of favor and courage that cancels out unnecessary fear and doubt.

I am thankful for my Throne Room and the freedom to manifest BLESSINGS and become ONE in You for those around me. In all faith, *As It Pleases You*, I submit to the Spiritual Journey of my Heaven on Earth Experiences to

The Cornerstone Prayer

become a Divine Vessel of hope, love, encouragement, and healing for the Nations. In Jesus' Mighty Name, I pray. Amen.

Throne Room 12

God's Promises Prayer

My Heavenly Father, from Genesis to Revelation, as You unveil the realities of Heaven, I come before You with a humble and open heart full of gratitude and thanksgiving in the Name of Jesus. O Lord, from the Divine Cornerstone of my faith, You are my Creator, my Sustainer, my Way Maker, and my Redeemer, and I would like to formally THANK YOU for the GIFT of Life. I want to take this moment to reflect on the big and small Blessings You have poured into my life, but one thing is for sure: Without You, there would not be me. So, I am ever so grateful for every breath I take, the blood flowing through my veins, for being in my right state of mind, and for allowing me to be Your child as I seek Your Divine Presence, *Spirit to Spirit*.

In my Relational Communion ordained from the Heavens Above, I acknowledge and understand that every good and perfect GIFT of my Divine Promises comes from You; therefore, I give You all the GLORY and REVERENCE in the Name of Jesus. In this moment of prayer, with Your Unconditional Love, I turn to You, my Heavenly Father, for Divine Wisdom, Supernatural Discernment, Godly Understanding, and a Spiritual Compass, navigating my every step with the Holy Trinity at the forefront.

In reflecting amid the Sheepfold of Your Promises as a child of the Most High God, I ask that You guide my Mind, Body, Soul, and Spirit as I circumnavigate the Vicissitudes, Cycles,

God's Promises Prayer

and Seasons of Life. Even when I am presented with challenges and uncertainties, when pruning the layers of ungodliness, unrighteousness, and anything unpleasing in Thine Eye, please become the Fourth Man in the fire, protecting and keeping me, my family, my loved ones, and anyone I hold dear to my heart from all hurt, harm, and danger in the Name of Jesus. Lord, as I cast down all fears, worries, and anxieties, I replace them with courage, peace, tenacity, and patience in You, allowing the Vicissitudes, Cycles, and Seasons to prepare me for Your Divine Timing.

Lord, as You uphold me with Your Righteous Hand, and as I move forward in the Spirit of Excellence, *As It Pleases You*, unveil my eyes to see people, places, and things from Your Divine Perspective. For I know Your Heavenly Thoughts are not like mine, and Your Divine Ways are not like mine, so I place a Spiritual Demand on Divine Understanding and Supernatural Wisdom from the Heavenly of Heavens. As I come before You in reverence, my Heavenly Father, supply all my needs according to Your riches in glory by Christ Jesus.

My Lord, as I seek to fulfill my Kingdom Responsibilities with Divine Favor, provide the Spiritual Oil flowing from the HEAD downwardly with an undeniable overflow permeating everything I touch. As the Heavenly Oil of Your Glory cascades over my life with compassion, for those willing to receive freely, soothe the brokenhearted, heal the sick, bring sight to the blind, restore the weary, mend the fractured, set the captives free, break every binding yoke unpleasing to You, and rejuvenate the Spirit Man, in the Name of Jesus.

As my reasonable service in Earthen Vessel, a Spiritual Conduit of Divine Mercy, graciously yields the Oil of Wisdom to assist me in rightly dividing and discerning properly, *As It Pleases You*. While, at the same time, weeding out the wolves in sheep's clothing and those who are lying on You and functioning with deceptive, evil, and negative measures.

God's Promises Prayer

In all things, when operating in Spiritual Principles, Standards, and Etiquette, allow Your Divine Oil to become a lamp under my feet and a Divine Light to my path to avoid wasting Your Precious Oil. As the Oil of Harmony flows through me, let the fire of Your Anointing ignite a thirst for You and Your Transformative Power.

Spirit to Spirit, as I trust in Your Divine Plans, Promises, and Provisions to facilitate my Predestined Blueprinted Mission, *As It Pleases You*, provide the Divine Illumination needed to utilize every stepping stone as preparation for my Cornerstone of Greatness. With the Divine Promise of hope, guidance, purpose, and assurance, allow me to go from self-aggrandizing satisfaction to doing, saying, and becoming *As It Pleases You*, my Heavenly Father. More importantly, as all things work together for my good, please help me to Spiritually Glean the underlying lessons, understandings, teachings, and messages with profound Spiritual Discernment, transforming my ordinary wisdom into Divine Wisdom.

In leaning not to my own understanding, may I lean on You, my Heavenly Father, for all the strength and endurance needed to operate and rise up like an eagle, soaring above in peace, precision, and poshness, encouraging myself and those around me. As I lift Your Name on High with the Divine Promises of Your unconditional love and unchanging nature, anchor me Mentally, Physically, Emotionally, Spiritually, and Financially with the Fruits of the Spirit to FEED, HEAL, BLESS, and ANOINT Your sheep. In doing so, as I hear, understand, prepare, deliver, or share Your Word, let the words of my mouth, the meditations of my heart, and the thoughts I think become Holy and Divinely Acceptable in Thine Eye. Meanwhile, as my tongue becomes the PEN of a READY WRITER in the Name of Jesus, soften my words with PURPOSE and PASSION from the Heavens Above. My Wonderful Counselor, with this Clarion Call from the

God's Promises Prayer

Heavenly of Heavens, I say to You, *Spirit to Spirit*, 'Speak Lord, Your servant is listening.'

In the Throne Room of Your Divine Presence, surround me, guide me, comfort me, and fill me with peace, patience, stability, and perseverance to live by example, *As It Pleases You*. In feeding Your sheep, O Lord, teach me how to seek You in every moment while behaving Christlike with excellent people skills, proactively filling the needs of Your precious flock. Moreover, my Heavenly Father, in a chaotic world filled with noise, insensitivity, confusion, unjustness, and unrest, let Your Divine Peace, which surpasses all understanding, guard my Mind, Body, Soul, and Spirit as You HEAL the Land of Promise as we UNITE in faith in the Name of Jesus.

Father, by the Blood of the Lamb, from the Old Testament to the New Testament, I reflect on Your Steadfast Promises of Divine Provisions with underlying cisterns, taking care of what belongs to You. For You are indeed my Shepherd, and in Divine Sustenance, I shall lack nothing as I call forth my Spiritual Negev and Manna from Heaven's Reservoir as Your Divine Justice permeates from Heaven to Earth.

Lord, in this Throne Room, Your Everlasting Mercy endures forever, and Your Word cannot lie, and as a Spiritual Covenant of the rainbow, You said that You would not destroy the Earth by water. So, with a heart for service, discipleship, and outreach, I plead with You today to help us avoid turning on ourselves or destroying ourselves with our idolatrous and demigod tendencies. For this reason, O Lord, I repent of all of my known and unknown proclivities, seeking Your Divine Forgiveness as I commit myself to be the Earthen Vessel used in the Divine Unveiling and Commission of Your 'Sheep to Shepherd Movement,' advancing Your Kingdom on Earth.

My Lord and Heavy Load Bearer, I embrace my Divine Right to the Supernatural Leading of the Holy Spirit and the Spiritual Redemption and Salvation from the Blood of Jesus,

God's Promises Prayer

with a Divine Peace that transcends all understanding. My Father, amid embracing Your Promises, *As It Pleases You*, help me to experience this Divine Peace in my heart, especially in moments of turmoil, deception, and distractions when being tripped up or blindsided. As I pinpoint my Divine Tribe, in the Name of Jesus, shield my mind from negative chatter, frustrations, and negative seeds, as You allow me to rest in the assurance that You are SOVEREIGN over all things.

With all of Heaven backing me while Spiritually Tilling my own ground, teach me to surrender my reservations and anxieties at Your feet, trusting that You are working all things for my good and Your Divine Glory. In embracing my Eternal Life Now in being fruitful and multiplying, *As It Pleases You*, PREPARE me to Prepare others, BLESS me to be a Blessing to others, RESTORE me to Restore others, HEAL me to become the Healer, and ENCOURAGE me to Encourage others, activating the Law of Reciprocity for the Greater Good in my Heaven on Earth Experiences.

As my life becomes the Ultimate Testament of Your Divine Presence and Glory, help me articulate and convey my words, thoughts, beliefs, and desires with a Heavenly Language coming from You, the Creator of them all. In addition, I need Your Divine assistance in positively penetrating the heart of mankind, making their creative baby leap from within with Divine Authenticity, Relevance, and Poshness, seasoned with the right amount of salt. Lord, as I become the Salt of the Earth, *As It Pleases You*, tantalizing the palates of those I encounter, lead me, guide me, prepare me, nudge me, and present me.

As I experience the Joy of Salvation in Christ Jesus, with the Heavenly Honey of Lovingkindness, my Lord, in the Spirit of Excellence, assist me in mastering my APPROACH and DELIVERY of all things Spiritual. My Lord, to ensure I do not lose sight of You in my extracting, converting, and flowing phases, make my articulating factors humbly smooth as

God's Promises Prayer

butter, easily understood, time-sensitively relevant, and extremely relatable, *As It Pleases You.*

In all of my endeavors and as Your Kingdom Triumphs in the Spirit of Reconciliation and for our Heavenly Banquet, whether I am accepted or rejected in all that I do, say, or become, allow my GOOD FRUITS to remain for the Greater Good. Meanwhile, positively impacting a multiplicity of the NEXT generation upon the NEXT until the end of time, preparing for the Bride of Christ, the Church.

In the Spirit of Expectancy and Readiness, I remain in Your Divine Fold as a faithful steward, bringing Your sheep into Divine Alignment, *As It Pleases You,* to do likewise. For the Divine Essence of the Bride is readily upon us for HOLINESS and DEVOTION of the arrival of the Bridegroom, allow Your Word to Divinely Penetrate the hearts of those with a willing ear to hear.

Lord, in the Richness of Your Glory, in closing this prayer of this Sacred Union, *Spirit to Spirit,* I am Yours, adorned in humility, obedience, and gracefulness, embracing the AUTHENTIC Spiritual Seal from the Heavens Above. My Heavenly Father, You are indeed the Alpha and the Omega, the beginning and the end...in the Spirit of Oneness, fill the hole in me with Divine Holiness. Better yet, as I stand in the Spiritual Gap in proxy, as a free-will offering, fill the hole in all Your willing vessels with the Presence of the Holy Spirit, covered by the Blood of Jesus, getting us to the right heart and mind postures, *As It Pleases You.*

Above all, as I take my Spiritual Seat at the Table for a time such as this, let no one or nothing stand in between us for Your GLORIOUS RETURN, in the name of the Father, the Son, and the Holy Spirit, I pray. Amen.

Throne Room 13

Combatting Selfishness Prayer

In this Throne Room, my Heavenly Father, in the Name of Jesus, I come before You with an open heart and mind on how to Combat Selfishness in a way that is PLEASING in Thine Eye. O Lord, with gratitude and reverence to You, the Most High God, I would like to take a moment to say, 'Thank You.' I thank You for being my Creator, sustaining my every breath and heartbeat as I remain in awe of Your Divine Greatness.

As you intricately weave my life together, going through the eye of a needle, I need Your Divine Presence, *Spirit to Spirit*, to deal with the elements of my known and unknown selfish traits flowing through my loins. My Faithful Guide and Way Maker, I seek Your Divine Wisdom in all that I do, casting down any negative residue of greed, self-centeredness, narcissism, entitlement, and conceit. Lord, wherever these character traits are hidden within my psyche, I uproot them right now, in the Name of Jesus.

In Light of the Kingdom of Heaven, may all of my decisions reflect Your Divine Righteousness. As I cast down self-seeking ambitions unpleasing to You, get rid of all of my insensitive thoughts, words, desires, habits, and behaviors as my conscience becomes a Spiritual Compass guided by the Holy Spirit. O Lord, as I cover myself with the Blood of Jesus, may my actions become a direct reflection of the Fruits of the Spirit with Christlike Character as You continually teach, mold, guide, and protect me.

Combatting Selfishness Prayer

During times of uncertainty, let me do nothing out of selfish ambition or vain conceit. Instead, O Lord, allow me to approach everything and everyone with outright humility with a Kingdom-Serving Mindset, *As It Pleases You*. In addition, when I am exhibiting self-absorbing behaviors, thoughts, or desires, nudge me to self-correct instantly to ensure that I do not stray from Your Righteous Path of Greatness.

As I am indeed a work-in-progress in Thine Eye, I proactively repent of any known or unknown Spiritual Errors, resentment, unrest, or negative harboring. While continuing to move forward in the Spirit of Excellence with a forgiving demeanor, clean heart posture, positive mindset, and renewed Spirit, I extend grace and compassion toward others, just as You have shown me.

Lord, as I unselfishly lift up those around me who are in need, I pray for the sick, I pray for the lonely, I pray for those who are hurting, I pray for the weak, I pray for the needy, I pray for the abandoned, I pray for those suffering great loss, I pray for the captives, I pray for the broken-hearted, I pray for those who are desperately challenged, and I pray for those who are struggling under the weight of the Vicissitudes, Cycles, and Seasons of Life. Lord, may Your HEALING HAND be upon them, providing comfort, love, peace, and restoration, confounding human understanding or reasoning. My God, in the Name of Jesus, please give them strength to persevere with a Supernatural Second Wind, only coming from You, my Heavenly Father. More importantly, in their darkest hours, O Lord, bring forth the Divine Illumination, Protection, and Assistance needed to usher in Heavenly Calmness, Support, and Encouragement to their weary souls.

In a time of division and strife, by Divine Decree, my Lord, as I am my brother's keeper, strengthen the worldwide bonds that UNITE us together as ONE with kindness, peace, and understanding. Above all, as we grow in faith, renewed and

Combatting Selfishness Prayer

restored, my Lord, let the Spirit of Unity rest upon us, Your precious sheep. As You are our Guiding Light, whether with family, friends, neighbors, strangers, or foes, grant us patience and grace to navigate the challenges we face together as ONE with respect and integrity, leading us back to the Kingdom of Christ Jesus.

Lord, You are my refuge and strength, an ever-present help in times of need or trouble, as my trials of today pave the way for a brighter path to my tomorrow. May my actions reflect Your Divine Love, Mercy, and Compassion, and in every encounter, let me be a Spiritual Ambassador of Global Unity with Divine Discernment, weeding out the wolves in sheep's clothing with the intent of conquering and dividing Your people. With all humility, Spiritually Equip me to recognize the selfish and insensitive falsehoods that threaten the Divine Unity of Your flock.

Lord, in Earthen Vessel, as I unselfishly suit up with my Spiritual Armor on my behalf and others, empower me with the Spiritual Tools and Wisdom to combat the negative, intrusive wiles of the enemy, seeing through deceptive measures and divisive tactics with total clarity, in the Name of Jesus.

In this Throne Room, *Spirit to Spirit*, let Your Divine Presence Reign in my life to seek the Greater Good, reflecting the Spiritual Essence of You to all I come in contact with. My Heavenly Father, may I find joy in the simple things in life to ensure I remain rooted and grounded in the people, places, and things that money cannot buy. More importantly, with each breath I take, may I draw closer to You while granting me the Divine Wisdom and Know-How to see the beauty in all things among the ashes.

In knowing that I am never alone, my Heavy Load Bearer, please help me to find and create a win-win out of a seeming lose-lose. I trust in Your perfect timing and Divine Plan for my life, so guide me in pinpointing the good in a not-so-good

Combatting Selfishness Prayer

situation to Spiritually Glean the lessons, understanding, and information needed to move forward in the Spirit of Excellence. My Lord, as You use me as an instrument of Your Divine Peace, grant me the Supernatural How-To on reverse engineering negative charactorial traits into positive ones, *As It Pleases You*, ensuring my positive fruits remain. In addition, my Loving Father, with a Spiritual Anchor from the Heavens Above, if I need to unlearn the behaviors that do not align with Your Divine Will, show me the way and what to do, step by step, as I confront them with courage, openness, and clarity.

As I grow in Supernatural Faith and Hope on my transformational journey with Your unwavering support, envelop me with the Holy Spirit and cover me with the Blood of Jesus, as You navigate my life as only You can do, *As It Pleases You*. In Jesus' name, I pray, Amen.

Throne Room 14

Healing The Land Prayer

My Heavenly Father, in the Name of Jesus, I come before You with an open, humble, and repentant heart, seeking Your Divine Grace, Mercy, and Strength. I acknowledge and respect the 'It Is Good' Declaration of the BEAUTY and GOODNESS residing in the land You have created, which is also within me. As I embrace Your Divine Truths, help me to foster a connection with You, people, places, things, and nature, *As It Pleases You.*

Lord, I know from the core of my being that the *Healing of the Land* begins within me to uplift, heal, and build, *As It Pleases You.* As I move forward in the Spirit of Excellence with Your Healing Touch, I cast down the scars of neglect, confusion, debauchery, pollution, regret, and sorrow that weigh heavily upon the land in which we live.

In *Healing the Land*, O Lord, as I am in Purpose on purpose, *As It Pleases You*, it is my time for Spiritual Rebirthing. On my fertile ground, it is my time to pluck up anything or anyone, including the weeds and tares that are not of You. According to Your Divine Will in my life, if anything or anyone is stunting my growth or development in You or for You, let it or them be removed, in the Name of Jesus, to *Heal the Land* inside of me with Divine Intervention and Illumination.

As I Spiritually Till my own ground in my Sacred Healing Process, grant me the wisdom and know-how to plant good

Healing The Land Prayer

seeds, producing good fruit in a multiplication fashion amid my Spiritual Rebirthing Process. In cultivating the fertile ground of my Mind, Body, Soul, and Spirit, allow the INDWELLING of the Holy Spirit to permeate every fiber of my being. In Earthen Vessel, allow Him to pluck up or prune anything or anyone that does not align with what is essential for *Healing the Land* inside and outside of me. Above all, I bind any known or unknown brokenheartedness, scars, scabs, or open wounds designed to beset me; therefore, I usher in the reversal process of Spiritual Dualism, setting me free from any form of unnecessary captivity or hemorrhaging.

By the Blood of the Lamb, in the Spiritual Cleansing Process for Divine Liberation and Fulfillment, I cast down any negative influences, thoughts, beliefs, words, traumas, habits, and desires, hindering my Spiritual Lessons for my transformational and renewal process from coming forth, *As It Pleases You*. Lord, I include the casting down of toxic relationships or unproductive habits, hindering our *Spirit to Spirit* Connection, while interjecting the positive aspects of them all, with no shame attached. In doing so, O Lord, provide a safe space for Supernatural Healing to occur from within me, spreading outwardly with an undeniable and effective impact from the Heavens Above.

My Father, in the Spirit of Oneness and Divine Alignment, it is time to heal me of all my infirmities, Mentally, Physically, Emotionally, Spiritually, and Financially, ushering in the Divine Wealth of the Kingdom, *As It Pleases You*. As my Spiritual Negev (My Underlying Reservoirs) run over, allow my overflow to engulf the lives of others as You BLESS me to be a Blessing to Your sheep and the Kingdom, in the Name of Jesus.

My Way Maker, as You build me up in Your Holy Presence with Divine Discernment, according to my Predestined Blueprint, break down and remove anything within me or outside of me that is not conducive to Your Divine Will for my

Healing The Land Prayer

life. Amid this Divine Unveiling process taking place within me, create in me a clean heart with the correct heart and mind posture. Renew a Righteous Spirit containing the Fruits of the Spirit with Christlike Character to uplift, inspire, nurture, and motivate others into Divine Greatness.

In calling forth the Heavenly of Heavens, in my self-mirroring, self-analysis, self-correction, missteps, and self-awareness process, I repent of all of my known and unknown unrighteousness, forgiving myself and others of all negative or debauched atrocities. Also, in my self-discovery phase, I release any form of resentment, hostility, hatred, or anger toward myself, others, or anything in between as I regraft my mindset and heart posture with acceptance, calmness, love, and rationality. As I become a work-in-progress, moving in the Spirit of Excellence without drowning out my conscience or inner voice, I decree and declare that all wailing tears and the inner landscapes of my psyche are replaced with tears of joy, peace, and reverence. While at the same time allowing my laughter to permeate my heart with cheerfulness from the Ancient of Days. By the Power of my Testimony, all of my mourning is now fully trained, prepared, and matured to become my time of dancing in my Heaven on Earth Experiences.

As the Blood of the Lamb and the harvest of Your Divine Goodness await Your Heavenly Presence, cover me with Divine Atonement, pruning back every branch that is not of You. As I emerge Spiritually Renewed, help me to gather up all of my stepping stones to build a Divine Cornerstone of Greatness, *As It Pleases You*. As I move around daily, please assist me in letting go of the now to embrace my Divine Next while moving forward in the Spirit of Excellence, embracing the lessons learned along the way.

In espousal of the Lion of Judah, *As It Pleases You*, for every seemingly lose-lose situation, circumstance, or event, help me to reverse engineer them into a Divine Win-Win with a work-

Healing The Land Prayer

in-progress mindset, heart-set, word-set, thought-set, desire-set, and mission-set pleasing in Your Divine Eye. Father, my God, in the Name of Jesus, with my cultivating courage from the Heavenly of Heavens, I embrace what or who is mine, and I formally release what or who does not belong to me, Spiritually Sealing the *Healing of the Land*.

My God, I know Divine Justice, Mercy, and Sovereignty rest in Your Divine Bosom; therefore, I take nothing for granted while giving thanks in all things, putting away all idolatry, pompousness, and disobedience. Upon entering my Promised Land, *As It Pleases You*, I put away my wandering or idealizing mindset of going back to Egypt, casting down all lingering thoughts, desires, laments, and tastes for the free comforts of fish, cucumbers, leeks, onions, and garlic. Father, in this Sacred Space, I know these are symbolically the secret ingredients of my own limitations and unfounded longings associated with jealousy, envy, pride, greed, coveting, and competitiveness, poisoning and contaminating my Mind, Body, and Soul. So, I bring these characteristics to a complete halt, saying 'no' to all of them. While at the same time, with clarity, I am also saying 'no' to the unnecessary Spiritual Struggles in the Name of Jesus.

In *Healing the Land* of my past, present, and future, I put all forms of discontentment behind me, removing all emotions, thoughts, desires, triggers, and words of dissatisfaction from my repertoire and replacing them with gratefulness, leaving room for my Heavenly Manna daily, taking one step at a time.

As I strive for a deeper understanding of You, my Heavenly Father, *Spirit to Spirit*, I look forward to embracing the Divine Covenant of Supernatural Provisions between You and my Forefathers, as I place a Spiritual Demand on what rightfully belongs to me at the right time, the right place, and with the right people. In addition, O Lord, as my Spiritual Gifts make room for me, setting me before men in high places, I embrace Your Divine Strength, Tenacity, and Endurance to embody the

Healing The Land Prayer

Spiritual Principles, making the seemingly impossible possible.

As the Spiritual Veil in my life is ripped from the top to the bottom, I pray that You mend the brokenness and traumas associated with the tearing away of people, places, and things that are not conducive to my reason for being. Lord, as communication has become more critical than ever, help me to set a guard over my mouth, knowing the right time to speak and when to hold my tongue, weighing my words accordingly.

As I become quick to listen, slow to speak, and slow to anger, let my tongue become the pen of a ready writer, especially when the Holy Spirit comes upon me with the power and authority to uplift, inspire, build, and bring life. Conversely, in striving to navigate my conversations wisely, I will not use my mouth to hurt, destroy, manipulate, or abuse myself or those around me. Instead, O Lord, grant me the unction to pause and reflect before engaging in a conversation to determine if it is ethically building or unethically tearing down, allowing my speech to become a powerful instrument of positivity, love, and hope.

In the Spirit of Oneness, allow love to pour out of my loins to bring peace and stability to those near and far, overriding the warring fears, regrets, and traumas of my very own psyche with forthrightness and courage. As I reel my thoughts, words, and desires in on a moment-by-moment basis with a Spiritual Reel, keep me on a straight and narrow path, accomplishing the God-Given tasks I was sent here to complete from the onset, unveiling the true beauty that lies within.

From beginning to end, as the Shepherd and Overseer of my soul, I give You all the glory, thanks, and honor. As I am in the Divine Sheepfold, I rejoice in Your Everlasting Mercy as You *Heal the Land*, in the Name of Jesus. For by His stripes, we are all HEALED with Hope and Purpose, striving to embody

Healing The Land Prayer

kindness, understanding, and righteousness in all that we do. Amen.

THRONE ROOM 15
Heaven's Language Prayer

My Heavenly Father, in the Name of Jesus, I come before You, seeking *Heaven's Language* from the Heavenly of Heavens, *As It Pleases You*. As I am filled with humility, awe, and reverence, I give thanks in all things, even if they do not appear pleasing to me. For this reason, I am asking that You open my Mind, Body, Soul, and Spirit to the Divine Language that SPEAKS from the HEAVENS ABOVE with love, mercy, kindness, understanding, and compassion for all mankind.

To become a beacon of light to feed Your precious sheep, Lord, I need You to speak to me, teach me, mold me, prune me, and lead me with the Presence of the Holy Spirit. As I listen with an open, willing, and obedient heart and mind posture, please cover me with the Blood of Jesus as I uplift and unite myself and others, *As It Pleases You*.

O' Lord, the Supernatural Power of seeking *Heaven's Language* in this Divine *Throne Room* is a part of my Spiritual Journey of my *Spirit to Spirit* Connection with You. In this place of prayer, worship, praise, and communion, I usher in the Divine Presence of the Holy Spirit into our Sacred Space. I also cover it with the Blood of Jesus as Spiritual Atonement for my Mind, Body, Soul, and Spirit. Wash me, O Lord, and cleanse me of all burdens, fears, and debauchery as I openly repent, seeking Your forgiveness as You renew my heart and

Heaven's Language Prayer

mind while strengthening me from the inside out in the Spirit of Righteousness.

As I embrace *Heaven's Language*, I invoke Your glorious Throne Room of everlasting Grace and Mercy, transcending beyond the limitations of my human dialect. I come before You with a humble heart and open mind, seeking the Divine Language from the Heavens Above to bring forth Divine Wisdom, Instructions, Understanding, Purpose, and Know-How. For You are the Divine Anchor of my Heaven on Earth Experiences; therefore, I long to understand and desire the Heavenly Expressions of Your unwavering Love, Favor, Peace, and Adornment.

Lord, open my Mind, Body, Soul, and Spirit to receive the Heavenly Whispers of Your Divine Words, Thoughts, and Desires coming straight from You. With Your Heavenly postured perspective, allow the Holy Spirit to help me in my known and unknown frailties and propensities. May Your Holy Spirit guide my thoughts, words, desires, emotions, and actions as You fill my soul with the Heavenly Communication that transcends earthly words, depictions, or disputes, polishing up my people skills, *As It Pleases You*.

My Father and Giver of Life, teach me to speak with the sighs too deep for words, to embrace the melodies of Your Divine Grace amid my Breath of Life that resonates in the Heavenly Realms. In expressing the inexpressible yearnings of my heart, please allow every breath I take to BREAK BREAD with You, my Bread of Life and Heavy Load Bearer. O Lord, I trust in Your faithfulness amid all of my daily challenges, desires, and goals, taking nothing for granted while giving thanks for all things.

When the weight of life gets heavy, I decree that You lighten the load by default, helping me to Spiritually Glean what I need to learn in order to grow, sew, and feed Your sheep as You BLESS me to be a BLESSING to others, in the Name of Jesus. My Lord, teach me to proactively see the needs

Heaven's Language Prayer

of those around me while giving me the courage, know-how, tenacity, and wisdom to respond lovingly and pleasantly with the proper home training and Spiritual Etiquette.

In my *Spirit to Spirit* Commitment to You, my Heavenly Father, I ask for clarity in my prayer life so that I may converse with You in the ways You desire, *As It Pleases You*. Help me to align my heart with Yours, embracing Your Divine Blueprint for my life. With an unadulterated Attitude of Gratitude, let the 'Manna' of my words reflect and encapsulate Your truth with no sorrow attached. Moreover, my Good Shepherd, allow my actions to resonate with Your Fruits of the Spirit as I become Spiritually Anchored in behaving Christlike in the Spirit of Unity and Oneness.

In being about my Father's Business, listening, learning, and digesting Your every word, *As It Pleases You*, may I experience the fullness of Your Divine Presence and the richness of *Heaven's language* to the HIGHEST. Let me be a Spiritual Vessel of Your Divine Light in Earthen Vessel, sharing the exquisiteness of Your Heavenly Message with those around me. With Your Unfailing Love grafting every fiber of my being, guide me in Spiritually Tilling my own ground to produce on a multiplying level uncommon to mankind. With this Supernatural Anointing, help me to activate the Law of Reciprocity on a level that can only come from You, my Heavenly Father.

In this Throne Room of *Spirit to Spirit* Communion, my motto is, 'Nobody but God Almighty!' I love You, I trust You, and I live for You...show me the Divine Way as I move forward in the Spirit of Excellence, doing what You have called me to do and feeding Your precious sheep with Divine Wisdom, Understanding, Relevance, and Simplicity. As my fears are replaced with faith, doubts with assurance, weaknesses with strength, and losses with wins, I chalk it all up and cover myself with the Blood of Jesus as the Holy Spirit illuminates my Spiritual Path to take my rightful place at the TABLE.

Heaven's Language Prayer

Father, as my Spiritual Oil flows from the Heavenly of Heavens, I thank You for inviting me into this Divine Communion with You. May I forever seek to dwell in Your Divine Presence and attune my heart to the Eternal Rhythms and Divine Downloads from the Heavens Above. In Jesus' Name, I pray. Amen.

Throne Room 16
Mental Astuteness Prayer

Father, my God, in the Name of Jesus, I come before You with a heart full of gratitude for the Gifts, Blessings, and Guidance You have bestowed upon me. With Your Divinely Extended Hand that is readily available to me, I humbly ask for Your Divine Guidance in sharpening my mind and enhancing my mental clarity to expand my territory, *As It Pleases You*. As I navigate through life, I pray that You shield and keep me from all hurt, harm, and danger, Mentally, Physically, Emotionally, Spiritually, and Financially, while cutting the cord on anything or anyone that is not of You, my Heavenly Father.

In a world filled with uncertainties and risks, with my Spiritual Protective Barriers from the Heavenly of Heavens, I am making a conscious effort to live by and through Your Divinely Written and Inspired Word, activating my Spiritual Senses and Compass. In developing my Spirit Man, *As It Pleases You*, I prioritize my self-awareness to recognize my self-induced limitations and vulnerabilities. In doing so, please assist me in making the appropriate assessments of situations, circumstances, events, and people posing potential dangers to my well-being or those around me.

By the Blood of the Lamb, I surround myself with individuals who respect me, uplift me, and challenge me in positive ways as I stand firm, protecting me and mine. For 'We' in TOGETHERNESS agree that no weapon formed against us will prosper, and every tongue unjustly rising

Mental Astuteness Prayer

against us shall be condemned in the Name of Jesus. As our Triple-Braided Cord tightens, *As It Pleases You*, provide us with a safety net and strong foundation to withstand the tests of time and the enemy's wiles to ensure Your Divine Will is done for our Heaven on Earth Experiences. In doing so, I polish up my people skills to communicate effectively and consistently with the Fruits of the Spirit at the forefront of our *Heavenly Language* to properly sustain our Cornerstone of Greatness.

In my moments of Sacred Stillness resonating deeply within me, or when in the hustle and bustle of life, when life is lifing, I come seeking clarity of mind in my Throne Room of Amazing Grace amid silence, pressure, and confusion, balancing them all. My Lord, please grant me the ability and capacity to see through the fog of doubt, misunderstanding, fear, scatteredness, and confusion. As I embrace calmness and focus, *As It Pleases You*, I allow my thoughts to flow freely, intentionally, positively, and purposefully with a full understanding of my thoughts, feelings, traumas, words, and weaknesses to steer clear of lies and distractions of the enemy. While at the same time allowing calmness to reign and clarity to emerge with the Heavenly of Heavens covering me with the Holy Trinity on high alert, protecting that which is already.

In reinforcing my faith and trust in You, O Lord, I pray that You would enlarge my understanding and give me Divine Wisdom and Intervention beyond my years. Please help me to approach challenges with discernment and to navigate decisions with Divine Insight and Illumination from the Heavens Above. May my thoughts be aligned with Your Divine Will, and may I see the world through the lens of Your truth with Divine Discernment, *As It Pleases You*. In recognizing that I am part of a larger tapestry woven by Divine Hands, I find comfort in the belief that my stepping stones are the steps needed for my Divine Training or Spiritual Classroom. All of which are directed toward FULFILLING

Mental Astuteness Prayer

my Divine Destiny for the establishment and placing of my Cornerstone of Greatness.

My Way Maker, as I center myself in You, develop my mind and heart posture with a desire for growth, uplifting, transformation, and influence, *As It Pleases You.* In acknowledging my human vulnerabilities, please protect me from confusion and doubt and grant me the courage to pursue knowledge, understanding, growth, sharing, and know-how while Spiritually Tilling my own ground. As I move forward in the Spirit of Excellence, let Your Divine Light Spiritually Illuminate my path, guiding me to make choices that reflect Your Heavenly Love and Adoration, according to my Predestined Blueprint.

As I seek Your presence, I also ask for Your hand to rest upon me, that I may grow in Divine Wisdom, Kingdom Stature, and in the ability to Spiritually Discern right from wrong, good from bad, just from unjust, and positive from negative, perfecting the Art of Spiritual Dualism. As the Divine Source of all Creation, I seek Divine Wisdom and Supernatural Understanding regarding the intricate interplay of Spiritual Duality. Lord, to avoid falling short in this area, strengthen my Mind, Body, Soul, and Spirit to understand the differences between equal and opposites. To multiply my seeds of Divine Growth for the Greater Good of all mankind, help me to transform, convert, and cultivate, *As It Pleases You*, with Divine Balance.

As I navigate the Spiritual Dualities of truth and illusion, peace and anxiety, winning and losing, faith and doubt, may my heart be filled with courage to face them all. Lord, grant me a double portion of compassion as my mind becomes filled with clarity so that I may serve You and others with the Spiritual Gifts You have given me.

To avoid becoming derailed from being about Your Kingdom Business, I strive to embody forgiveness and repentance at all times, allowing me to rise above my past,

Mental Astuteness Prayer

present, and future grievances to remain in a constant state of healing, *As It Pleases You*.

    I turn to You, engaging in my *Spirit to Spirit* Connection, and I say, 'Thank You, Lord' for hearing my heartfelt prayer for *Mental Astuteness* and Clarity, *As It Pleases You*. O Lord, I open my heart and mind to new Heavenly Perspectives with a Resilient Spirit and Unwavering Faith, trusting in Your Everlasting Goodness and Your Predestined and Perfect Plan for my life with Blessed Assurance, in Jesus' Name. Amen.

Throne Room 17

Newness of Greatness Prayer

My Heavenly Father, in the Name of Jesus, as I stand at the threshold of a new chapter in my life, I humbly seek Your Divine Guidance, Understanding, and Wisdom. I thank You for the Predestined Assignments You have given me and for the Spiritual Lessons I have learned on my journey thus far. Now, as I usher in the Newness of Greatness, I ask for Your Divine Presence to envelop and cover me beyond human reasoning or understanding.

Lord, as I usher in the Holy Spirit, *As It Pleases You*, instill in me the Spirit of Courage and Hope as I embrace the challenges and tasks ahead. My God, in the Name of Jesus, help me to have and maintain the confidence, boldness, and tenacity needed for Your Divine Plan of Greatness, knowing that each step I take is Spiritually Guarded, Guided, and Protected by Your Everlasting Loving Hand.

May my heart posture be open to receive the opportunities You lay before me, and my mind be filled with clarity and understanding to discern Your Divine Will for my life. In addition, please help me to calibrate my Spiritual Compass to discern the wolves in sheep's clothing, dream killers, guised liars, gift-sucking leeches, time wasters, and destiny predators. In doing so, O Lord, I give You all the glory and thanks for the nudges, red flags, and alerts coming from the Heavens Above. Amid all, govern my words to become smooth as butter and sweet as honey to deal with them

Newness of Greatness Prayer

accordingly, provoking their conscience to speak to them about their debaucherous efforts. More importantly, if any of these negative attributes reside within me, I reverse them into positive attributes that are pleasing to You.

By the Blood of the Lamb, I pray for supernatural strength to overcome obstacles and issues, contending with every cycle that is not of You. In addition, I also pray for the grace to be a vessel of Your Divine Love and Light, bringing forth good fruit in multiplication form. May I approach this new assignment with joy, love, peace, patience, kindness, goodness, faithfulness, gentleness, self-control, enthusiasm, and a deep sense of purpose, while exhibiting Christlike Character and excellent people skills. My Heavenly Father, let me be ready to serve others, bringing goodwill and compassion into every situation, *As It Pleases You.*

My Lord, in Earthen Vessel, may my actions, reactions, thoughts, beliefs, desires, and words reflect Your Divine Glory in my Heaven on Earth Experiences. Fill me with unwavering faith and the assurance that with You, all things are possible, when Spiritually Tilling my own ground, *As It Pleases You.* In Jesus' Holy Name, I pray. Amen.

Throne Room 18

Self-Awareness Prayer

Father, my God, in the Mighty Name of Jesus, I come before You with a humble and contrite Spirit, seeking Your Divine Guidance in becoming self-aware of my words, thoughts, beliefs, desires, habits, and actions, or the lack thereof. As we are all created in Your Divine Image, I take full responsibility for the image I place before Your Heavenly Throne, *Spirit to Spirit.* At the same time, O Lord, based upon the Unconditional Love You have for me, I am making a willing and conscious attempt to reflect deeply on the essence of who I am from the inside out. In taking this leap of faith to take a deep dive within my psyche, *As It Pleases You*, peel away the negative layers of debris and false expectations that I have allowed the world to place upon me to cloud my true self, fogging up my sense of good judgment.

My Heavenly Father, as I seek to reflect on the core of my being, *Spirit to Spirit*, with each step of my Spiritual Journey, help me to engage in the self-examination process through the lens of Your Word. Please grant me the courage and tenacity to unveil the parts of myself I prefer to deny, hide, or project on others. In doing so, I am also asking You to place Divine Introspection where I can truthfully assess my psyche's desires, unrestrained entrapments, and unresolved yearnings. O Lord, as I grow closer to You, *Spirit to Spirit*, and more in tune with my Divine Purpose or reason for being, I understand that

Self-Awareness Prayer

I am also accountable for my fruits and the management of them to become a new creation, *As It Pleases You*, according to 2 Corinthians 5:17. For this reason, O Lord, I need the correct information from the Heaven's Above regarding the intricate tapestry that makes me who I am and what causes my Mind, Body, Soul, and Spirit to jump the track, making it UNPLEASING to You invoking a Spirit of Disdainment.

My Lord and Savior, in the same breath, while engaging in reflective efforts in this Sacred Exploration Phase, *As It Pleases You*, I need You. Yes, my Lord, I really need the Presence of the Holy Spirit in the EXTRACTING and CONVERTING process, turning my shortcomings into opportunities for positive growth and transforming my losses into win-wins for the Greater Good. My Heavenly Father, as I engage in self-examination or self-awareness according to Your Word with the Spiritual Principles, Etiquette, and Poshness needed to acknowledge my strengths and weaknesses, help me to become a bona fide work-in-progress with Divine Clarity, Wisdom, and Understanding. Meanwhile, soberly assessing myself, *As It Pleases You*, getting rid of the Spirit of Harshness, Meanness, Unkindness, Messiness, Rudeness, and Disorderliness.

In examining my heart and mind posture, O Lord, please help me to understand the underlying or unresolved behaviors, habits, traumas, stunted growth, and emotional woes derived from my psyche or whatever is hidden under something else that is not conducive to my well-being. In recognizing my Spiritual Need to become a better version of myself, *As It Pleases You*, my Heavenly Father, today, I repent of all of the known and unknown animosity I have caused, created, or whitewashed. I also repent for exchanging wisdom for foolery and debauchery, and now I am seeking peace and understanding in my progression, not superficial perfection with zero progress.

Self-Awareness Prayer

As I seek forgiveness, *Spirit to Spirit*, in the Name of Jesus, help me to work my way up to obtaining Divine Wisdom from the Heavenly of Heavens with the Spiritual Fruits to sustain my Spiritual Status in the Kingdom. As I learn to accept my flaws with a positive mindset, I formally surrender to my Predestined Blueprint and Your Divine Will for my life with outright HUMILITY and OBEDIENCE with an eagerness to learn, understand, grow, share, and sow back into the Kingdom when called upon.

My Lord, in becoming Self-Aware and attuning to Your Divine Guidance, *As It Pleases You,* I cast down the **Spirit of Jealousy**, replacing it with the Spirit of Freedom, Acceptance, and Trust. My Lord, I am seeking Your Divine Guidance and Strength in overcoming the Spirit of Jealousy that has taken root within me over people, places, and things belonging to me. I will no longer allow any perceived threats to negatively affect my relationships, connections, decisions, and self-perception. For this reason, O Lord, I remix any lingering insecurities, unresolved fears, lingering possessiveness, undealt with suspicions, prolonged paranoias, unresolved resentment, and hidden anxieties with the Courage of the Kingdom.

Any personal experiences, conditional upbringing, and societal influences attempting to keep me yoked or soul-tied, I break them right now, in the Name of Jesus. I break any factors associated with mistrust, emotional distance, controlling actions, and destructive behaviors as I cover all of them with the Blood of Jesus, washing me clean of all negative impurities as I embrace the positive aspects of life.

In becoming Self-Aware with an eagerness to Divinely Glean from the Reservoir of Wisdom, *As It Pleases You,* I cast down the **Spirit of Envy**, replacing it with the Spirit of Contentment, Calmness, Confidence, and Security. My Lord, I am seeking Your Divine Guidance and Strength for an undisturbed mind in overcoming the destructive forces

Self-Awareness Prayer

associated with negatively influencing my thoughts, actions, words, and reactions about people, places, and things not belonging to me. By the Blood of the Lamb, I remove all feelings or insecurities dealing with self-doubt, inadequacy, discomfort, resentment, or distorted views. My Lord, any feelings, emotions, or thoughts producing malicious envy, including any attempts to undermine, badmouth, or sabotage the envied person, I remove them right now, in the Name of Jesus.

In this Throne Room of Grace, to embrace my hope, *As It Pleases You*, I repent of any atrocities caused by my engagement in toxic relationships. In addition, I also repent of all my ungodly situations, mistrusting hostilities, envious suspicions, unjustified connections, conditionally oriented disconnections, or outright looking for dirt to slander, trapping me in a cycle of negative emotions. Forgive me, O Lord, of all of my self-seeking, evil-speaking, or selfish desires as You help me to become Kingdom-Seeking and Kingdomly Selfless.

From this point onward, I only want and seek what belongs to me, *As It Pleases You*, and according to my Predestined Blueprint, in the Name of Jesus. For this, O Lord, I need Divine Clarity to Spiritually Discern what is truly meant for me and what is not. In addition, I am requesting the Divine Wisdom and Patience needed to wait for the proper timing without succumbing to fleeting desires or counterfeits. As I navigate this path, Divinely Synchronize me with You, *Spirit to Spirit*, to ensure we operate with ONE heart and mind with the Spirit of Contentment, being satisfied with what You provide, knowing You do not make mistakes.

In becoming Self-Aware and renewing my mind, *As It Pleases You*, I cast down the **Spirit of Coveting**, replacing it with the Spirit of Selflessness, Unassuming Contentment, Internal Satisfaction, Unresounding Gratefulness, and an Ongoing Appreciation for You, myself, and others. My Lord, I am

Self-Awareness Prayer

seeking Your Divine Guidance and Strength in overcoming the deep longings and desires, particularly for something or someone that belongs to someone else, be it material possessions, traits, achievements, relationships, or anything in between. As I recalibrate my moral compass into that of the Kingdom, please help me to set realistic and relevant boundaries, Mentally, Physically, Emotionally, Spiritually, and Financially.

From this point onward, my Lord, in echoing Your Divine Essence in my life, I will no longer keep up with the Joneses' heart postures, mindsets, or demeanors. So, I am making a willful decision to cast down all of my unfulfilled needs or desires from within, be it known or unknown. In addition, I also cast down anything or anyone invoking a sense of inadequacy or negative emotions from within me, diminishing my self-worth, attacking my self-esteem, or straining my relations with You, myself, and others.

My Lord, my goal is to keep up with the Kingdom and my Divine Purpose, *As It Pleases You*, building my Mind, Body, Soul, and Spirit with positivity, gratitude, and contentment. Therefore, I repent of all negativity contributing to anything or anyone fueling the elements of dishonesty, manipulation, or exploitation, causing me to lose value in my achievements, desires, know-how, and the Spiritual Gifts lying within my loins. Any source of conflicts associated with jealousy or envy leading to any sort of coveting and discontentment unpleasing to You, O Lord, I cancel it right now in the Name of Jesus. Instead, I replace this negative condition with UNITY, LOVINGKINDNESS, and CONTENTMENT in the Spirit of Excellence.

My Lord, with the Divine Assistance of the Holy Spirit, help me to recognize that my identity and worth are rooted IN YOU, not in what I possess or lack. More importantly, above all else, grant me Spiritual Discernment to see the Spirit of Coveting in myself. O Lord, with a Spiritual Mirror, first,

Self-Awareness Prayer

unveil my eyes to see the Fruits of Coveting to ensure I can self-correct at the drop of a dime. Secondly, *Spirit to Spirit*, help me to proactively correct the deceptiveness designed to distract me or steal my peace, joy, and sanity as You FIX the hole in me, *As It Pleases You*.

My Lord, in the hole hidden deep within my psyche, please heal the known and unknown wounds that have led me to look outwardly for validation. Teach me to trust in Your Predestined Blueprint, as I work diligently to find my self-worth anchored IN YOU and Your Divine Will. Above all, O Lord, as the Holy Spirit fixes the glitch in my system, show me how to transform my negative feelings into positive feelings and fervent prayers of gratitude for what I have. While, at the same time, in the tapestry of my existence, I am GRATEFUL for what I do not possess positively or negatively and for the time-sensitive Divine Provisions of what I do not have as of yet.

My Heavenly Father, whatever state I am in, I thank You for the LESSONS learned and TRIALS faced in and out of my Spiritual Classroom, both in my times of abundance and in my moments of lack. As the Divine Presence of the Holy Spirit guides me in being present in each moment, *Spirit to Spirit*, I trust in the Divine Unfolding of my true self for the Greater Good when the time is right. In the meantime, I am Spiritually Tilling my own ground in preparation, *As It Pleases You*.

In becoming Self-Aware and when seeking to hear Your Voice, *As It Pleases You*, I cast down the **Spirit of Arrogant Pride**, replacing it with the Spirit of Humility, Respectfulness, Submissiveness, and Servitude. My Lord, I am seeking Your Divine Guidance and Strength in overcoming while cleansing my heart and renewing my mind, *As It Pleases You*. O Lord, free me from having a dismissive attitude toward others that hinders me and damages my relationship with You and others. Moreover, please help me to deal with the underlying fears or inadequacies causing me to desire outright control or to feel

Self-Awareness Prayer

self-important, covering up my hidden feelings of self-doubt that go unspoken about, covered up, or undealt with in Thine Eye, *As It Pleases You.*

In this Throne Room, *Spirit to Spirit*, I am laying my negative character traits on the table...I will no longer project man-made and orchestrated confidence. My Lord and Heavenly Father, I am committed to becoming Divinely Confident IN YOU from the inside out with Divine Wisdom, releasing the pressure of having to play pretend.

- ☐ In dealing with the Spirit of Arrogant Pride, I will no longer be condescending. Instead, I will become humbly encouraging, helpful, and motivating, using my words and behaviors to uplift without dividing, build without tearing down, or motivate without hindering, seasoning my words with salt and the delivery of them as smooth as honey, *As It Pleases You.*

- ☐ In dealing with the Spirit of Arrogant Pride, I will no longer be unapproachable or feared. Instead, I will become down-to-earth and authentically relatable, listening and celebrating others while remaining on a continuous learning curve, *As It Pleases You.*

- ☐ In dealing with the Spirit of Arrogant Pride, I will no longer turn up my nose at those appearing less than. Instead, I will become understanding and compassionate to the differences or conditions of others with a balanced approach, *As It Pleases You.*

- ☐ In dealing with the Spirit of Arrogant Pride, I will no longer initiate conflict among peers, friends, family members, or foes to offend or upset them. Instead, I will defuse conflict by bringing peaceful words,

Self-Awareness Prayer

thoughts, actions, and resolutions into my relations with all I come in contact with, *As It Pleases You.*

- ☐ In dealing with the Spirit of Arrogant Pride, I will no longer be a stiff-necked individual in Your Eye. Instead, I will become humbly obedient, listening, learning, understanding, and growing to become a better person daily with a work-in-progress mindset, *As It Pleases You.*

- ☐ In dealing with the Spirit of Arrogant Pride, I will no longer be considered dull and lacking enthusiasm. Instead, I am committing myself to work on my people skills to become a better communicator, fostering trust and respect, *As It Pleases You.*

- ☐ In dealing with the Spirit of Arrogant Pride, I will not become dismissive of the thoughts, ideas, and cultures of others. Instead, I am developing a free-will mindset, allowing people to be who they are. At the same time, I will *Live by Example* and as a *Living Testimony* in the Spirit of Excellence, increasing the morale of those I encounter, *As It Pleases You.*

- ☐ In dealing with the Spirit of Arrogant Pride, I will no longer be the toxic one in the group. Instead, I will become the Go-To or the Problem Solver, instigating creativity, openness, and progress, *As It Pleases You.*

- ☐ In dealing with the Spirit of Arrogant Pride, I will not block feedback. Instead, I am open to correction and valuable insight to become better, stronger, and wiser in all that I do, say, and become, *As It Pleases You.*

Self-Awareness Prayer

My Heavenly Father, help me to internalize Your Divine Truth deeply within my soul, recognizing the distractions and fleeting feelings associated with the Spirit of Arrogant Pride, designed to subtly lead me away from You or away from my Predestined Blueprint. Lord, fill me with the Holy Spirit and cover me with the Blood of Jesus so that I may resist the temptations and snares leading me astray. As I reflect Your Divine Love and Grace on a moment-by-moment basis, may I rise each day with renewed determination to walk boldly in the LIGHT, while You lead me in the Path of Righteousness for the Kingdom's Sake.

In becoming Self-Aware and Spiritually Transformed from the inside out, *As It Pleases You*, I cast down the **Spirit of Greed**, replacing it with the Spirit of Generosity, Thankfulness, Selflessness, and Charity. My Lord, I am seeking Your Divine Guidance and Strength in overcoming the insatiable desire for more, more, more without being grateful or content with what I already have, and becoming a good steward of them. From this day forward, O Lord, I will no longer be bound by the fear of scarcity or being left behind. I will no longer be soul-tied to deep-rooted insecurities, known or unknown inadequacies, and a desire for validation from anyone or anything outside of You, my Heavenly Father, as I cut the cord right now on this debilitating behavior, in the Name of Jesus.

In addition, I cover with the Blood of the Lamb the bar that is continuously moving higher and higher due to my known and unknown ungratefulness, perpetuating my secret dissatisfactions and the underlying restlessness hidden within my psyche. In nipping the Spirit of Greed in the bud, O Lord, I will not become consumed with striving to outdo another. Nor will I prioritize my desires over ethical considerations, contributing to unethical behavior, corruption, resentment, division, or exploitation. As You Divinely Mold me into a VESSEL of Your Divine Grace, I put

Self-Awareness Prayer

away anything or anyone, causing the Spirit of Ungratefulness, Discontentment, or Negativity to rear up within my loins with a double-edged sword. As You are my Witness, I will become a Cheerful Giver, a Cheerful Teacher, and a Cheerful Sharer, activating the Law of Reciprocity for the Greater Good on behalf of the Kingdom of Heaven while aligning my ambition with selflessness, helpfulness, compassion, mercy, and sustainability, *As It Pleases You.*

In becoming Self-Aware and developing Spiritual Discernment, *As It Pleases You*, I cast down the **Spirit of Competitiveness**, replacing it with the Spirit of Teamwork, Cooperation, Unselfishness, Uniqueness, and Supportiveness. As my heart beats in rhythm with Yours, I will no longer mislead myself with false comparisons of others, as my Predestined Blueprint should never match another. Nor will I vainly pit myself against another or one person against another. Instead, I will unite with others with common goals to become better, stronger, and wiser, *As It Pleases You.* In Your Divine Eye, You made me unique; therefore, I will only compare myself with myself, according to the Spiritual Blueprint from within, while learning from everything and everyone to become better, stronger, and wiser for the Greater Good.

In becoming Self-Aware and remaining Spiritually Focused, I cast down the **Spirit of Confusion**, *As It Pleases You*, replacing it with the Spirit of Peacefulness, Understanding, Harmony, and Unity. My Lord, as a beacon of sustaining hope, I am seeking Your Divine Guidance and Strength in overcoming the Author of Confusion. For this reason, I place the Holy Trinity at the forefront of the Spiritual Quaternity of the FOUR CORNERS of my Mind, Body, Soul, and Spirit to bring forth Divine Equilibrium from the Heavens Above.

In becoming Self-Aware, *As It Pleases You*, O Lord, I cast down the lust of the eyes, the lust of the flesh, and the pride of life, freeing myself from the idolatrous efforts and the negative

Self-Awareness Prayer

influences associated with the hunger for power, the love of money, sexual promiscuity, and manipulative control. By Divine Authority in the Name of Jesus and *As It Pleases You*, I replace all of them with Supernatural Power, Heavenly Provisions, Chastity, Divine Usability, and Godly Influence for the Greater Good.

My Heavenly Father, based on the Spiritual Law of Seedtime and Harvest, may my life's harvestable harvests become a Testament to the internal freedom of the Gift of Cognitive Self-Awareness, as my Testimonies impact lives for the Greater Good, bringing forth much good, positive FRUITS.

My Lord, as I pass these Spiritual Fruits to the NEXT in line, I am committed to feeding Your precious sheep, *As It Pleases You*. Lord, I recognize that these Fruits—love, joy, peace, patience, kindness, goodness, faithfulness, gentleness, and self-control—are not merely attributes to be displayed but GIFTS to be shared. Therefore, my Heavenly Father, I am asking that You help bring forth the Christlike Character Traits that are PLEASING to You. When I share these Spiritual Fruits, I pray that I do so with a Spirit of Generosity and cheerfulness to deepen and establish my own walk with You, in the Name of Jesus.

In moving forward in the Spirit of Excellence, may my actions, thoughts, beliefs, desires, and words serve as a mirror of Your love, drawing others closer to You, *As It Pleases You*. Let them all be seasoned with grace, empathy, and love, bringing comfort to the traumatized, weary souls and hope to the downtrodden or broken-hearted.

As I am Spiritually Backed by the Heavenly of Heavens, based on the Spiritual Covenants or PROMISES You made to my Forefathers, the Tribe of Judah, and to those who are willing to become ONE with You, *Spirit to Spirit*, we will leave no WILLING vessel or sheep behind. For, indeed, we are all

Self-Awareness Prayer

deserving of Your Divine Love. In the Name of Jesus, I pray. Amen.

Throne Room 19

Spiritual Fruits Prayer

My Heavenly Father, in the Name of Jesus, I step into my Sacred Space and Throne Room of Grace, approaching You with deep gratitude, humility, and reverence. Lord, as You have given me this day, I give it back to You, *Spirit to Spirit*, allowing it to do what You have designed it to do. Amid all things, as I stand in awe of You, open my eyes and cover me with the Blood of Jesus while allowing the Holy Spirit to go before me, clearing my path to Spiritual Maturity and Growth. As I anchor my faith, trust, and reliance in You, gleaning the Divine Wisdom this day is generously offering me, I become like a Spiritual Sponge, soaking it all up to pour out when I am squeezed, *As It Pleases You*.

Lord, as I embark upon my Spiritual Journey with a humble heart and open mind to You, allow Your Divine Grace and Mercy to penetrate every fiber of my being. My Heavenly Father, I ACKNOWLEDGE and come into AGREEMENT with my Fruits of the Spirit from the deep pits of my loins. I place a Spiritual Demand on them to come forth, sprouting from the very depths of my being, where You have intentionally planted my seeds of Love, Joy, Peace, Patience, Kindness, Goodness, Faithfulness, Gentleness, and Self-Control.

Lord, as I dig deep for the Divine Emergence, allow the Divine Whispers of the Holy Spirit to nudge, stir, and direct my corrective efforts in cultivating and refining what is

Spiritual Fruits Prayer

already in my DNA, *As It Pleases You*. In reshaping me into an Earthen Vessel that radiates Kingdom Poshness, please grant me the tenacity and grace to move forward in the Spirit of Excellence. As I embark on this transformative, fruitful journey with a work-in-progress mindset, allow the words of my mouth, the meditations of my heart, and the thoughts of my mind to become Holy and Righteous in Your Divine Eye.

In all things, my Heavy Load Bearer, grant me the patience to endure challenges while feeding Your sheep. In addition, my Lord, I need Christlike kindness to serve them with clean hands and a pure heart, along with the proactive know-how in displaying the appropriate or relevant character traits needed for the moment. In my Divine Authenticity, *As It Pleases You*, let my interactions with others become a Heavenly Reflection of You, in the Name of Jesus.

In surrendering to Your Divine Guidance, Will, and Provisions as I strive to grow, sow, and multiply in Kingdom Principles, Standards, and Etiquette, prune anything that is not according to Your Divine Plan. If it or they do not Spiritually Align, *As It Pleases You*, remove it or them as I humbly press the release button to reset my Mind, Body, Soul, and Spirit to bear my Spiritual Fruits in accordance with You, my Heavenly Father.

In deepening my understanding of the Fruits of the Spirit, I would like to take a moment to THANK YOU for the precious GIFT of the Holy Spirit, who guides and empowers me in The Way, according to Your Divine Will and Predestined Blueprint. Lord, as You allow the Fruits of the Spirit to manifest and change me for the Greater Good in Earthen Vessel, transform my words, thoughts, beliefs, and desires into Spiritual Attributes, bringing GLORY to the Kingdom, in the Name of Jesus.

My King of Kings and Lord of All, in gaining a Spiritual Understanding, *As It Pleases You*, I need You. When reflecting on my Spiritual Fruits and Traits, one by one, help me to

Spiritual Fruits Prayer

embrace the Spirit of Love, which is the primal foundation of all of my Spiritual Fruits and Character Traits. In Infinite Wisdom, with this motivational and securing foundational factor associated with my Heaven on Earth Experiences, I am reminded that Your understanding far exceeds my own.

My Redeemer, to ensure I am anchored in love, peace, and purpose, I pray that You teach me how to love unconditionally, transparently, selflessly, and sacrificially, *As It Pleases You*. While at the same time heightening my Spiritual Discerning Faculties to ensure I do not become a victim of abuse, trauma, misuse, or fall for the okey doke. As a Spirit yearning for growth, deliver me from situations having the potential to sow negative, deceptive, or debauched seeds of misuse, coercion, discord, and manipulation.

Above all, in the Name of Jesus, guard my heart against the allure of underlying or low-hanging fruits of temptation, silent acts of disobedience, false intentions, or outright idolatry. In addition, O Lord, open my Spiritual Eyes to see beyond the surface level of what is presented, along with the Spiritual Ears to hear what is not being said, the Spiritual Tongue to speak without offense, and the Spiritual Unction to know when it is time to back up, step up, step down, or shut it down altogether.

Amid my deep compassion for loving those who may or may not be difficult to love, my Heavenly Father, grant me the Supernatural Wisdom and Understanding on how to effectively communicate with Agape (Unconditional Love), Platonic (Non-Romantic Love), Familial (Family Love), Storge (Parent-Child Love), Ludus (Playful Love), Eros (Passionate Love) Pragma (Long-Term Love), Xenia (Hospitality Love), In knowing the difference, *As It Pleases You*, with this free will choice of love and regardless of the reciprocation, I Divinely Invoke the PROTECTION of my sanity, heart posture, and well-being with an impenetrable Spiritual Covering on HIGH, safeguarding my other Spiritual

Spiritual Fruits Prayer

Fruits and self-love used to feed Your flock of sheep. In doing so, Lord, help me to weed out all forms of Infatuational Love with the potential of leading to the wolf in sheep's clothing Mania (Obsessive Love), underlying Lustful Love, and outright soul ties designed to taint my Spiritual Fruits and Divine Love.

Lord, with my service-oriented Kingdom Mindset, I extend proactive repentance and forgiveness on my behalf, atoning for my known and unknown sins, mishaps, and quirks. Also, I extend this same grace to that of another to ensure my heart is free of any lingering, debauched residue. For this reason, I cast down anything or anyone attempting to prevent me from heeding the Divine Call of my Heavenly Father. Moreover, my Wonderful Counselor, I am getting out of my own way, so whatever bad fruits are in need of purging, I release them to the Spiritual Purging and Regrafting Process.

When it comes to the out with the old and in with the new mindset, I rebuke anything or anyone inhibiting my understanding of the depth and breadth of Divine Love. I silence anything or anyone with negative distractions, voices of doubt, and negative influences, attempting to thwart my ability to exude the Spirit of Joy, *As It Pleases You*. I invoke the Lion of Judah against anyone or anything, trying to cloud my heart and mind with unwise or foolish rhetoric and distractions to zap my courage or violate my free will.

In doing my part, *As It Pleases You*, my Heavenly Father, my goal is to foster an environment of acceptance, healing, inspiration, and unity, uplifting the downtrodden or fallen. My Deliverer, in a world filled with challenges, hate, hostility, chaos, confusion, and division, I reverse all of them into opportunities, calmness, peace, understanding, and oneness in the Name of Jesus. Lord, I pray that You grant me joy on a level uncommon to the human repertoire, drawing me closer to You, *Spirit to Spirit*, while remaining Kingdomly Usable. As I find my Spiritual Joy (my deep-rooted sense of contentment

Spiritual Fruits Prayer

and fulfillment) in You, please allow this Divine Gift to overflow into the lives of others, impacting all I encounter as a Divine Testament to Your FAITHFULNESS and PROVISIONS.

In this sacred moment, as I seek my Divine Birthright of peace, by the Spiritual Power vested in me, I cast down all negative anxieties, fears, worries, and doubts, attempting to zap my tranquility. My Lord, my Heavenly Father, I acknowledge You as the Creator of all things, the Divine Source of true tranquility from the Heavens Above. I know You are in control of every situation, circumstance, or event that I will face on my unpredictable journey, dealing with a myriad of experiences, challenges, and opportunities containing the Divine Wisdom I need to glean. Thus, I am asking for Divine Guidance in bringing peace to my Mind, Body, Soul, and Spirit first, as I lay everything and everyone at Your Divine Feet. And then, I ask that You bring peace surpassing all understanding to my home, workplace, and community, even with decision-makers and everywhere my feet trod in Christ Jesus.

As I encounter the Vicissitudes, Cycles, and Seasons of Life, Lord, grant me the patience needed to do what needs to be done and say what needs to be said, in the Name of Jesus. Where there is tension in my life, O Lord, I pray for release, prioritizing peace over conflict. Where there is known or unknown sickness, grant Supernatural Healing in the Name of Jesus. Where there is an obvious or misconstrued misunderstanding, provide Divine Clarity, Wisdom, and Instructions. Where there is brewing or underlying anger, provide Heavenly Calmness, smiting the Spirit of Anger at its root. By the Blood of the Lamb, where there is hatred, please provide the elements of Spiritual Love, breaking all types of strongholds and chokeholds to provide Divine Liberation. Where there is unforgiveness, Father, my Lord, bring about forgiveness, soothing the psyche of all I encounter. Where

Spiritual Fruits Prayer

suffering is occurring in war-torn regions, for those displaced by violence, and for those who live in fear, bring forth Divine Peace and Deliverance in the Name of Jesus.

As I pray for worldwide peace, teach me to wait on You, understanding that Your timing is perfect as I persevere in hope, anchoring my mind on things that are pure, lovely, upright, and praiseworthy. Moreover, may I also proactively extend Supernatural Patience to others, fostering understanding, kindness, and compassion in all their known and unknown interactions.

Father, fill my heart, mind, and conversations with kindness, allowing my gentle and caring demeanor to come forth while treating everyone with respect and dignity. Lord, I also pray for help in proactively seeing the needs of others and responding willingly, spreading Your Divine Love through my actions, reactions, thoughts, and words while fellowshipping with others. Then again, in the manifestation of the Fruits of the Spirit, *As It Pleases You*, this also applies when engaging in acts of service, when dealing with challenges, when surrendering to Your Divine Will, when feeding Your sheep, when being about Your Business according to my Predestined Blueprint, or when operating in the Spirit of Goodness.

Lord, I pray to embody the goodness attributes of integrity, righteousness, and a commitment to doing what is right in Your Divine Eye to become a Living Testimony, giving and receiving goodness from the Heavens Above. Nonetheless, in my Good-Spirited interactions, decisions, and responses, please help me maximize Spiritual Dualism to discern good from evil, right from wrong, positive from negative, just from unjust, and to choose paths that honor You.

As I embrace my Divine Calling, *Spirit to Spirit*, let my actions demonstrate Your everlasting goodness, and may I become LIGHT in a dark world, providing Divine Illumination to those who are veiled to the TRUTH of Your

Spiritual Fruits Prayer

Word. In faithfulness to You, my Divine Mission, and my relations with others, I am standing firm on my commitment to You and feeding Your precious sheep. I will also endure my trials and temptations as my training ground for my NEXT and as my preparation to pass the Divine Mantle to the NEXT in line.

In the advancement of the Kingdom, *As It Pleases You*, my Heavenly Father, grant me gentleness of speech, action, reaction, and interaction with myself and others. Lord, as I continue to humbly Spiritually Till my own ground for growth, maturity, and advancement amid the Spiritual Principles of Seedtime and Harvest, help me to multiply with the Law of Reciprocity. While simultaneously exhibiting kindness, one to another, producing Good Fruits and Abundant Harvests that are UNDENIABLE.

Father, in Divine Obedience to building the Framework and Wall of Greatness with the Fruits of the Spirit, *As It Pleases You*, I ask for self-control to govern my desires, habits, lusts, senses, impulses, and most of all, my tongue. In addition, I reject anything or anyone that would cause me to become a city with broken-down walls due to a lack of self-control. Lord, allow me to use self-control as a protective barrier in order to feed Your sheep properly with the MILK and MEAT of Your Word. For this reason, I need Divine Knowledge and Wisdom to develop the discipline and discernment in turning away from all temptations, lies, debauchery, and selfishness to focus on what is pure, truthful, and righteous in Thine Eye.

Above all else, in clinging to what is good, effective, and productive, in or out of the Kingdom, by Divine Decree, I put away and cast down all forms and triggers of **JEALOUSY** pertaining to what seemingly belongs to me. In stomping out the Spirit of Jealousy, I remove all elements of selfishness, entitlement, and violating the free will of another. Any negative thoughts or feelings of insecurity invoking this emotion, I will cancel them immediately and replace them

Spiritual Fruits Prayer

with something positive, productive, and fruitful, in the Name of Jesus. According to Your Word, I can do all things through Christ who strengthens me. So, with Your Divine Help, I bring forth selflessness, humility, gratefulness, and security from the inside out.

In Divine Declaration, I disengage from all forms and triggers of **ENVY** associated with what does not belong to me. In eradicating the Spirit of Envy, I shift my focus to wanting and creating the best for everyone, even if they do not want it for themselves. In freeing myself from the internal burdens and consequences of envy, with Your Divine Assistance, O Lord, I will build, inspire, encourage, and lend a helping hand to those who are in need of what I have to offer for the Greater Good, according to my Predestined Blueprinted Mission.

In Divine Assertion, I eradicate all forms and triggers of known and unknown **PRIDE** lingering in my Mind, Body, and Soul. In removing the Spirit of Pride, I will only operate in the Spirit of Humility. Even if people think that I am weak, let it become my greatest strength, hidden in plain sight, that makes a POWERFUL statement in and out of the Kingdom. As I surrender my ambitions, hopes, and dreams to You, *As It Pleases You*, let my words, thoughts, actions, beliefs, desires, and reactions become the Salt of the Earth with a Heavenly Savor while becoming sweet as honey and smooth as butter simultaneously.

In Divine Proclamation, I eliminate all forms and triggers of **GREED** from my loins. In removing the Spirit of Greed, I come against the lust of the eyes, the lust of the flesh, and the pride of life. Instead, with the Holy Trinity at the forefront, I activate the Law of Reciprocity to give, give, give, and share, share, share to coax a sense of connection and fulfillment from within. On a broader scale, my Heavenly Father, please help me to become content in whatever state I am in, laying to rest all forms of idolatry, fear of scarcity, addiction to clutter, or prolonged discontentment.

Spiritual Fruits Prayer

In lifting the Spiritual Veil through self-awareness and self-analysis, I am getting rid of all forms and triggers of **COVETING**. O Lord, in bringing the Spirit of Coveting and the fear of missing out to a complete halt, by Divine Decree, I usher in the Spirit of Contentment and Gratefulness. With the Fire of the Holy Spirit, I come against and sever ties with whatever fear, trauma, loss, or lack lingering from within, causing the Spirit of Lust to manifest itself with the desire to want things belonging to someone else. According to Your Word, You have not given me a Spirit of Fear, but of POWER, LOVE, and a SOUND MIND. From this point onward, I lay claim to this Spiritual Seal from the Heavenly of Heavens. While I trust in Your Divine Timing, first, I only want what You, O Lord, want for me, *As It Pleases You*. Secondly, I want what rightly belongs to me, and I lay claim to my Promises, Inheritances, and Birthrights in the Name of Jesus.

In Divine Proactiveness and Assertiveness, I remove all forms and triggers of **COMPETITIVENESS**. I cast down the Spirit of Competitiveness and Comparison, leading to destructive rivalry and confusion. By the Blood of the Lamb, I will only compete with myself, aligning my Heaven on Earth Experiences, *As It Pleases You*, and according to my Divine Blueprint, with a deeper drive to improve, excel, and inspire myself and others in the Spirit of Excellence. I will not operate in the Spirit of Perfection, lacking humility or failing to test my actions, underlying motives, mental chatter, and heart posture. Instead, I will operate with a work-in-progress mentality, leaving room for continual growth daily to broaden my knowledge and understanding, adding to my repertoire of Divine Wisdom to carry my own load. With this approach, O Lord, help me to become mentally better, internally stronger, and more confidently astute to share my knowledge and experiences to build and refine myself and others with resilience and perseverance according to Kingdom Principles and Standards.

Spiritual Fruits Prayer

Finally, my Sovereign King and Way Maker, in Spiritual Readiness, *As It Pleases You*, I strive to embody the Fruits of the Spirit. As a Fruitful Believer, I give thanks in all things, the good, bad, and indifferent, recycling my formerly rotten fruits into Spiritual Fertilizer (A Testament or Testimony) for my VIRTUOUS FRUITS. May I seek to Divinely Glorify You and Your Everlasting Name in all that I do, say, and engage in as a Spiritual Ambassador of the Kingdom. In Jesus' name, I pray. Amen.

Throne Room 20

The Good Shepherd Prayer

Father, my God, in the Name of Jesus, I come before You seeking Your Divine Guidance, Strength, Mercy, and Comfort. As I am in the Throne Room of Your Divine Presence, *Spirit to Spirit*, I would like to take a moment to pause, reflect, and give thanks for Your Everlasting Greatness.

My Heavenly Father, *The Good Shepherd*, the Divine Creator of it all, with Your Divine Care and Compassion for me, I give praise and homage to You for Your unwavering and unadulterated love that endures forever. As You feed, nurture, and cover me, thank You for being my refuge and my strength, a present help in my moments of trouble, unsurety, and unrest. O Lord, I am grateful for the myriad of Divine Blessings, Leadership, and Guidance You have poured into my life, even in moments of aloofness or when I am veiled, not being able to recognize them.

My Way Maker, as I exude the virtues of love, sacrifice, selflessness, and responsibility, please help me to remain focused and steadfast while navigating the complexities of life. Lord, You said that You are *The Good Shepherd*, and You know all the intricate aspects of my being; therefore, I surrender all to You, *As It Pleases You* and *Spirit to Spirit*. With all the choices and challenges that lie ahead, I seek Your wisdom and clarity as the word of my mouth, the meditations

The Good Shepherd Prayer

of my heart, and the thoughts of my mind become Holy and Acceptable to You, my Lord, my Strength, and my Redeemer.

As I move forward in the Spirit of Excellence, *As It Pleases You*, help me to Spiritually Discern Your Divine Will, Nudges, and Internal Gravitational Pull toward leading Your precious sheep while being about Kingdom Business. In embracing the Divine Path or Predestined Blueprint that You have set before me, I pray for the clearing of clutter, Mentally, Physically, Emotionally, Spiritually, and Financially. May my heart be open to Your Divine Voice of Reason, Instruction, Guidance, and Wisdom as the manifestation of my Spiritual Courage and Protection comes forth as the Lion of Judah, following Your Divine Lead.

Moreover, in times of uncertainty, I know that I am never alone. In this moment with You, my Good Shepherd, please carry me on Your shoulders as Graceful Redemption becomes my portion in the Name of Jesus. By the Blood of the Lamb, in the same way that a normal shepherd cares for their sheep, I trust that You are watching over me, caring for me as I want for nothing while lying in green pastures. Amid my soul being refreshed and restored by You, my Heavenly Father, grant me peace and sanity beyond human understanding with the ability to think on my feet, making the right moves at the right time, and remaining still when necessary.

Lord, I also pray for the strength to face threats, ambushes, deceptions, distractions, and trickery, knowing when to hold, when to fold, and when to walk away in the Spirit of Calmness and Resilience without revealing my hand or playing myself short. To the Most High God, with my hands lifted toward the Heavens Above, please replenish my Mind, Body, Soul, and Spirit with the vital Spiritual Nutrients to sustain my strength and vision. All of which allows me to soar like an eagle with extraordinary acuity to see clearly across all distances, Mentally, Physically, Emotionally, Spiritually, and Financially.

The Good Shepherd Prayer

With sharpness in my thoughts, clarity in my Divine Purpose, and navigating my emotions with forgiveness, grace, understanding, and wisdom, my heart and mind posture will rise above anything and anyone that is not of You, my Heavenly Father. In addition, regardless of what I see or what I am faced with in or out of the SHEEP FOLD, help me to rise above discouragement, debauchery, or disillusionment with my eyes fixed on You, my ultimate Source of Hope.

In my relationships, Lord, grant me the grace to exude the Fruits of the Spirit while behaving Christlike at all times, speaking and behaving kindly to myself and others while Leading by Example and Spiritually Tilling my own ground, doing what I am called to do. My Lord, as I interact with family, friends, and even strangers, let Your Divine Love shine through me, providing the necessary illumination needed to lead them back to the Kingdom, *As It Pleases You.* When they see me, they will also see You as I become an excellent orator and listener with an understanding, compassionate, and merciful heart with Supernatural People Skills, feeding Your sheep as my tongue becomes the pen of a ready writer.

Amid the issues we face in my community or challenges in the world, I bring them before You, *The Good Shepherd.* I trust in Your Perfect Plan and Divine Timing, knowing that You are always at work, even when I cannot see it. As You heal the brokenhearted, setting the captives free, may Your Divine Peace and Healing permeate my community and the world with Blessings upon Blessings and Miracles upon Miracles, surpassing all human understanding in the Name of Jesus.

Lord, my Rock and my Fortress, I pray for a Spirit of Gratitude and Comfort to fill my heart daily as You Bless me to become a Blessing to another. As the sheep of Your pasture, I see the beauty in the small things and acknowledge Your hand in every moment. While at the CENTER of Your Throne Room, help me to turn negative situations into positive ones, turn bad situations into good ones, and turn a lose-lose into a

The Good Shepherd Prayer

win-win with a work-in-progress mindset, leading me to the SPRING of Living Water, wiping away every tear.

As my faith and hope deepen with You, the Chief Shepherd, may I walk in Your Divine Ways all the days of my life with the Spiritual Unction to function, *As It Pleases You.* Finally, as I humbly stand before You, Heaven is my Witness, and according to the fulfillment of my Predestined Blueprint, I ask that You unveil everything I need to bring forth the Divine Greatness with the unfading Crown of Glory, feeding Your precious sheep. In Jesus' Name, I pray. Amen.

Throne Room 21

Tree of Life Prayer

My Heavenly Father, in the Name of Jesus, I humbly come before You today, seeking Your Face in the Realm of the Spirit as my heart overflows with a good theme of gratitude and gratefulness on high, *Spirit to Spirit*. My Lord, the Illuminating Light from the Ancient of Days, I thank You for this moment in time, which is a PRECIOUS GIFT to me, filled with Your Divine Love and Compassion. As I commit my day to You, my Lord, do with it as You please, as I attune my heart and mind to Your Heavenly Voice, All-Knowing Instructions, and Divine Intervention.

Spirit of the Living God, in this Sacred Space, with Your Heavenly Goodness and Mercy at the forefront, I take nothing for granted. I cherish every breath You have granted me, inhaling and exhaling with reverence for the name above all names, Yahweh. With Your Divine Presence connected to every breath I take, I am reminded of Your Divine Handiwork encoded, precoded, and decoded within my DNA. As the Tree of Life is within the core of my being, I breathe in deeply, calling upon the INDWELLING of the Holy Spirit. My Lord, with each inhalation, I welcome in Your Divine Presence, Peace, and Wisdom, and with each exhalation, I release my known and unknown burdens, fears, mishaps, worries, failures, and traumas into Your Divine Hands.

My Lord, as Your Divine Wisdom whispers to me, *Spirit to Spirit*, I pray that You guide and govern my words, thoughts,

Tree of Life Prayer

desires, emotions, beliefs, and reactions, *As It Pleases You*, to calm my known and unknown internal qualms or storms raging from within. In order to become a Testament to Your Divine Greatness, here is what I need to do:

- ☐ With my Tree of Life, I turn confusion into clarity.
- ☐ With my Tree of Life, I reverse hatefulness into lovingkindness.
- ☐ With my Tree of Life, I transform my bad fruits into good ones.
- ☐ With my Tree of Life, I turn uncertainty into hope.
- ☐ With my Tree of Life, I reverse doubt into faith.
- ☐ With my Tree of Life, I transform fear into courage.
- ☐ With my Tree of Life, I reverse engineer lack into abundance.
- ☐ With my Tree of Life, I turn stuntedness into growth.
- ☐ With my Tree of Life, I transform my loneliness into companionship.
- ☐ With my Tree of Life, I reverse engineer lose-loses into win-wins.
- ☐ With my Tree of Life, I convert all negatives into positives.
- ☐ With my Tree of Life, I turn my deflection into self-reflection.

Straight out of the Divine Gate, when dealing with Spiritual Dualism, as You and I walk together in Divine Agreement, *As It Pleases You*, I formally place a Spiritual Demand on Your Divine Wisdom. My Lord, in acknowledging the profound truth found in Your Word, You said that Wisdom is a Tree of Life, and happiness is a result of those who retain her. For this, O Lord, I embrace this Wisdom Promise wholeheartedly, and I lay claim to my Spiritual Portion of Wisdom, in the Name of Jesus.

Tree of Life Prayer

As a child of the Most High God, let my Tree of Life in its wholeness, my Roots in their totality, and my leaves in their multiplying fullness GROW STRONG from the soil of Your Word. In addition, may they all become fertilized by Your Spiritual Fruits, where there is NO LAW against their usage. Nevertheless, amid my Seedtime and Harvest Phase, *As It Pleases You*, allow my Spiritual Fruits that are Divinely Connected to my Tree of life to become healthily nourished by my consistent thankfulness, my unwavering prayerfulness, my constant forgiveness, my continuous repentance, my non-stop mercifulness, and my meditational reflections.

As I stand firm in Your Divine Presence, I know that You are the foundation of every fiber of my being, designed to provide a source of encouragement, hope, comfort, guidance, and support for me and Your sheep in Earthen Vessels. My Lord, in the All-Seeing Eye of my Creator, as Your Divine presence watches over me, my family, my TRIBE, and all that I hold dear to my heart, I acknowledge Your Omnipresence, *Spirit to Spirit*. Amid Your Heavenly Watchfulness, also keep Your Divine Eye on all of us, helping us to develop an interconnectedness as Spiritual Beings first, branching upwardly toward You, our Heavenly Father.

As I reflect on this Sacred Knowledge and Understanding, please help us to become rooted downwardly, Divinely Interlinking our Heaven on Earth Experiences in the Spirit of Oneness, developing a strong intrinsic connection to one another in a community of faith, love, and hope like a Triple-Braided Cord, *As It Pleases You*. In the multitude of safety with the Lord of All Creation, weave our lives together with PURPOSE and INTENTION with our hands lifted up toward the Heavens. In addition, as a Spiritual Safety Net, we need Your help in respecting our unique differences while recognizing the common thread that unites the Tree of Life within us all through Your Son, Jesus Christ. For In Whom,

Tree of Life Prayer

bruised the heel of the enemy for the Divine Right I am Spiritually Enforcing, *Spirit to Spirit*.

In the broader tapestry of my existence and triad of strength in the Holy Trinity that cannot be easily broken, I walk in unwavering togetherness with You, my Heavenly Father, *Spirit to Spirit*. Whether I am branching upwardly or becoming rooted downwardly, I invoke a Divine Sense of BALANCE between my Mind, Body, Soul, and Spirit for growth personally, privately, openly, and Spiritually. My Lord, Abba Father, I am leaving absolutely no stone unturned in preparation for my Predestined Blueprinted Mission, *As It Pleases You*. From the Ancient of Days, as You Spiritually Illuminate my path, grant me the Divine Discernment to recognize and apply Your Divine Truth or Revelation accurately and succinctly. In addition, my Heavy Load Bearer, please help me to Spiritually Detect what an outright lie in Thine Eye is or is not, how to deal with it or them, and in what manner to respond accordingly, even if it does not require one.

My Lord, in the Sacred Light of Your Heavenly Gaze from Heaven to Earth on Your Divine Terms, I pray that You show me the way into Your loving arms, resting in Your Heavenly Bosom under Your Infinite Wing, *Spirit to Spirit*. Abba, my Father, as I am filled with hope, strength, and resilience, bring forth the Tree of Life already hidden within my loins to walk uprightly with You. Moreover, I need Your Divine Guidance to avoid unwise paths of foolery, to strategically evade sitting in the seats of the scornful, or entertaining wolves in sheep's clothing without foreknowing who they are, what I am dealing with, and who sent them. At the same time, I am suited up with Spiritual Armor and Tools, keeping my composure with a straight, unadulterated face with Supernatural Self-Control. Above all, my Lord, grant me the Divine Discerning Faculties to read my Spiritual Fruits and their fruits accurately with a Bionic Lens from the Heavenly of Heavens, as I behave Christlike with excellent people skills,

Tree of Life Prayer

not allowing my left hand to know what the right hand is doing, while still moving forward in the Spirit of Excellence, in the Name of Jesus.

My Lord, in my Throne Room, I make a formal commitment to growth, pruning, connection, and sharing with a work-in-progress mindset in my Spiritual Phase of Seedtime and Harvest. Based upon the Law of Reciprocity of Spiritually Tilling my own ground and putting my hands to the Spiritual Plow, may my Spiritual Roots of Kingdom Fitness become deeply intertwined with Kingdom Principles, Standards, and Protocols, *As It Pleases You*.

In laying Spiritual Claim to my Rights of Dominion to my Tree of Life for my Heaven on Earth Experiences, let no weapon formed against me prosper, and every tongue rising up against me in this Divine Phase of Righteous Fruit Development shall be condemned, in the Name of Jesus. *Spirit to Spirit*, I do not play around with my Tree of Life, my Spiritual Fruits, or my Supernatural Leaves, for with Spiritual Wisdom, all of my pruned limbs, rotten fruits, and dead leaves are strategically designed to become the FERTILIZING Testimonial Nutrients for the NEXT Generation, with a multiplying cycle for the Greater Good feeding Your precious sheep.

Lord, my Merciful Father, in the FRUITFULNESS and MULTIPLYING cycle of goodness and positivity in Earthen Vessel, *Spirit to Spirit*, I gather in Your Divine Presence, embracing the Predestined Blueprint of my Tree of Life. In doing so, *As It Pleases You*, I am seeking Heavenly Peace, Divine Understanding, Supernatural Wisdom, and Unfailing Guidance from the Holy Spirit while covering myself with the Blood of Jesus. In the Spirit of Obedience, while at the Table of Showbread, as a Spiritual Vessel of the Most High God, it is my reasonable service to use my Spiritual Fruits to feed Your sheep with the Bread of Your Presence in multiplicity form for

Tree of Life Prayer

the Greater Good, allowing the leaves of my Tree of Life to become used for the HEALING of the Nations.

My Lord, I pray that You cultivate my Spiritual Roots, nourishing not only myself but also those around me, fostering an environment of love, support, forgiveness, compassion, and unity with the RIGHT Materials, Dimensions, Designs, Placement, and Maintenance that are Spiritually Marked and Sealed from the Heavens Above for my TRIBE. Amid all, when life is lifing, I refuse to become a Tree of Death and Destruction, especially when there is so much PROMISE hanging in the balance. Therefore, in light of Your Divine Love, Mercy, and Provisions set forth from the Beginning, I lay claim to what rightly belongs to me, in the Name of Jesus, as You provide the Divine Nourishment and Soil needed to facilitate my Spiritual Evolution, IN YOU.

As I stand under the watchful Eye of my Heavenly Father, O Lord, remove the blinders from my eyes and unclog my ears to ensure I can hear You clearly, correctly, and consistently, reinforcing Revelation 2:7: *"For He who has an ear, let him hear what the Spirit says to the churches. To him who overcomes I will give to eat from the tree of life, which is in the midst of the Paradise of God."* More importantly, set a guard over my tongue, knowing when to speak, when to remain silent, and when to avoid perverseness, as my tongue becomes the pen of a ready writer for the Kingdom with a DIVINELY ORDAINED Supernatural and Direct Connection to the Heavenly of Heavens with a Heavenly Language surpassing human reasoning.

As I pause to reflect on the significance of my Sacred Tree, O Lord, I am grateful for the Spiritual Fruits that my Tree of Life bears as I cultivate my own ground. By the Blood of the Lamb, as I become Spirit-Filled, *As It Pleases You*, here is what I Spiritually Declare and Decree:

☐ My Lord, I Declare and Decree I am a Tree of Love.

Tree of Life Prayer

- ☐ My Way Maker, I Declare and Decree I am a Tree of Joy.
- ☐ My Shepherd, I Declare and Decree I am a Tree of Peace.
- ☐ My King of Kings, I Declare and Decree I am a Tree of Patience.
- ☐ My Lord of Hosts, I Declare and Decree I am a Tree of Kindness.
- ☐ My Loving Father, I Declare and Decree I am a Tree of Goodness.
- ☐ My Savior, I Declare and Decree I am a Tree of Faithfulness.
- ☐ My Comforter, I Declare and Decree I am a Tree of Gentleness.
- ☐ My Creator, I Declare and Decree I am a Tree of Self-Control.

In the Spirit of Wisdom, as the Mantle of the Holy Spirit is upon me, may I strive to embody these Christlike Qualities and Kingdom Etiquette, *As It Pleases You*. Doing so ensures my life aligns with Your Divine Will with Spiritual Fruits positively impacting those around me, bringing the much-needed Spiritual Edification to the Nations, as You PROMISED.

As I move forward with the *Tree of Life* inside of me, instill in me a clean heart, renew in me a right Spirit, a passion for service, an authentic desire to uplift, build, and encourage, and the wisdom to lead Your precious sheep with humility. Lord, may I never forget or downplay the weight of my responsibility to You, myself, others, and the Kingdom of Heaven.

As Your Divine Mercifulness restores and heals us, let our abundant GOOD FRUITS reflect Your Divine Glory, as You ignite desire to serve You in Spirit and in Truth. As I step forward in faith as a good steward, I surrender my will to Your

Tree of Life Prayer

Divine Will, *As It Pleases You.* May my life be a TESTAMENT of Your Divine Love, Grace, and Mercy, positively impacting lives for generations to come. In the Name of Jesus, I pray. Amen.

Throne Room 22
Unveiling Instincts Prayer

My Heavenly Father, in the Name of Jesus, I come before You with a humble heart and mind posture, seeking to deepen my understanding and connection to the Divine Essence of who You are, *Spirit to Spirit*. My Lord, I recognize that within me resides a SACRED GIFT of Instincts. Yes, my Heavenly Father, I am referring to those little gentle nudges and weighty feelings that guide my path and shape my choices that You Divinely Planted inside of me. As You grant me the courage to develop my inside voice, I am asking on this day that You UNVEIL the WISDOM embedded within my instinctual nature.

In Divinely Unveiling my Spiritual Instincts and Perception, *As It Pleases You*, I come before You with my hands lifted toward the Heavens. As I approach Your Throne Room of Grace, allow the Presence of the Holy Spirit to come upon me, opening the door to Your Heavenly Presence, *Spirit to Spirit*. At the same time, unveiling Your Divine Wisdom one to another, leading and guiding me in the Spirit of Righteousness, casting down all doubt, fear, and frustration.

My Lord, it is through Christ Jesus that I have Divine Access to You; therefore, as I align with Your Divine Will for my life, I place a Spiritual Demand on what rightly belongs to me, and that is Your Everlasting Presence. My Heavenly Father, in living authentically and purposefully, I Spiritually Awaken and Align myself to become ONE with the Holy

Unveiling Instincts Prayer

Trinity, inviting Divine Revelation to come forth, *As It Pleases You.*

O Lord, as I trust in You with all my heart, mind, soul, and every fiber of my being, I ask that You unveil my Spiritual Instincts already pre-coded within my DNA, clearing all of my Mental, Physical, Emotional, and Spiritual cobwebs. In doing so, grant me the strength, know-how, and unction to embrace Your Divine Wisdom and the Supernatural Power to realize, comprehend, appreciate, and engage my Divine Purpose as I lean not to my own understanding.

My Heavy Load Bearer, by the Blood of the Lamb, and as I submit to You, please instill in me a clarity that transcends human comprehension, allowing me to recognize Your Divine Guidance in all things while making my path straight and undeniable. May my Spirit be open and receptive to the unfailing truth, and may the love of Your Divine Light Spiritually Illuminate my path for me to lead Your precious sheep authentically, transparently, and effectively.

My Lord, help me to trust and comprehend Your Predestined Blueprinted Plan, ensuring I do not deceive myself into thinking I am more than I ought. In addition, I need Your Heavenly Assistance in discerning good from evil, truth from falsehood, right from wrong, just from unjust, positive from negative, Godly from ungodly, and so on, mastering Spiritual Dualism, *As It Pleases You.*

In moving forward in the Spirit of Excellence, please grant me the courage and tenacity needed to grow in faith, *As It Pleases You,* satiating all fears and doubts attempting to sift me away from Your Divine Presence, in the Name of Jesus. As the Creator of all things, fill me with the knowledge, insight, foresight, and discernment required to navigate the complexities of life with grace, mercy, and love.

In Earthen Vessel, amid the Cycle, Vicissitudes, and Seasons of Life, prepare me, test me, prune me, re-graft me, mold me, grow me, multiply me, and lead me with the Divine

Unveiling Instincts Prayer

Greatness that can only come from the Heavens Above. As I invoke the Law of Reciprocity, I activate Your Divine Word, placing it at the forefront of my life, cutting through anything that is not of You. As I seek Your Face, my Heavenly Father, I need Your Divine Guidance and Wisdom to navigate through my thoughts, actions, and emotions to Spiritually Regulate them to ensure negativity and rebellion do not creep into the crevices of my Mind, Body, and Soul.

O Lord, as I place my hope and assurance in You, my Heavenly Father, fill me with the Fruits of the Spirit, allowing Love, Joy, Peace, Patience, Kindness, Goodness, Faithfulness, Gentleness, and Self-control to permeate my life to ensure I reflect Your Divine Grace and Mercy through living by example. While becoming more Christlike, *As It Pleases You*, create in me a clean heart and renew in me a right Spirit, guiding me toward Divine Peacefulness, Unwavering Unity, and Divine Timing for my Heaven on Earth Experiences, allowing my stepping stones to become Spiritual Cornerstones.

My Bread of Life and Way Maker, I thank You for Your unfailing Divine Presence, Covering, and Support as You guide my thoughts, desires, and postures to dwell on what is pure, lovely, and praiseworthy. Lord, You are my refuge, my fortress, my stronghold, and the all-knowing, steady hand that undergirds and guides me through every challenge, including the ups and downs. May I always find Supernatural Comfort and Peace in Your Divine Presence, *As It Pleases You*, reflecting the depth of Your Everlasting Mercy, and the Divine Joy of Your PROMISES.

On this day, before Your Throne, I surrender my doubts, fears, or all negative thoughts, desires, and inclinations to You. In exchange, I embrace my Spiritual Journey in Earthen Vessel, while being confident in the Supernatural Strength, Tenacity, and Wisdom You have so graciously bestowed upon me. As a servant of the Most High God, fill me with the desire

Unveiling Instincts Prayer

to serve others, *As It Pleases You*. In Jesus' Holy Name, I pray. Amen.

Throne Room 23
Walking In The Word Prayer

My Heavenly Father, in the Name of Jesus, I come before You with a humble heart, *Spirit to Spirit*, seeking Your Divine Presence, Guidance, and Daily Bread. In this Throne Room of Grace, I thank You for Your unfailing love and for allowing my Spiritual Compass to come forth, providing an internal roadmap to lead me in the Path of Righteousness, *As It Pleases You.*

    Lord, amid the hustle and bustle in life, I desire to walk in Your Word, allowing it to be the Guiding Light, leading me step-by-step with Divine Revelation, Supernatural Growth, Uncommon Wisdom, Superfluous Comfort, and Heavenly Understanding. As Your Word becomes a Spiritual Lamp under my feet and an Advocating Light to my path, Divinely Illuminate the way, bringing light to my darkest moments and making them great and transformative, *As It Pleases You.*

    As I immerse myself in Your Word, I align my thoughts, decisions, desires, words, beliefs, and actions according to Your Divine Will. O Lord, it is my reasonable service to submerge myself completely in Scripture while meditating on them day and night, developing my heart and mind posture for the Greater Good and Kingdom Business. More importantly, grant me the ability to become a Living Epistle of Your Word, applying it in every aspect of my life and living by example.

Walking In The Word Prayer

My Lord, by the Blood of the Lamb, I place a Spiritual Demand on knowing and living the Word, *As It Pleases You*, to Spiritually Till my own ground and fulfill my reasons for being. As I seek to fulfill the Predestined Mission You have proactively designed for me, I ask for Divine Clarity and Discernment in hearing Your Voice, *Spirit to Spirit*, in the Name of Jesus. Above all, in my intimate moments of my Heavenly Downloads, please reveal my Spiritual Gifts, Tools, and Principles needed to facilitate whatever I need to do and with whomever, bringing me into Divine Alignment in the Spirit of Obedience, Peace, and Joy.

As the Deliver of my Mind, Body, Soul, and Spirit, use all of me for Your Divine Glory, inspire me with Your Spiritual Classroom teachings to ensure I am properly trained, nurtured, tested, and ready, *As It Pleases You* with the Spiritual Discipline, Principles, and Astuteness of the Kingdom. My Lord, as my Spiritual Discernment faculties remain cued up and ready to go, please assist me in recognizing opportunities, the ways in which I can serve others, and the simplest ways to become a beacon of light in my community or for the next in line.

According to the Heavenly of Heavens, I am created in Your Divine Image to do good works, *As It Pleases You*; therefore, with the Divine Reassurance of Your Word, empower me to step boldly into the rightful calling You have set before me, feeding Your precious sheep.

Lord, as I experience a taste of Heaven on Earth, I pray for obedience in my heart and discipline of my mind to trust You in every situation, knowing that Your Divine Plans for me are good, pleasing, and perfect with no shame attached. Strengthen my faith, hope, and tenacity as I invoke my Spiritual Filtering Process of self-correcting, self-analyzing, self-control, and self-actualizing amidst the noise of the world to avoid any form of self-deception or self-induced trauma. My Heavenly Father, while truth and freedom prevail in my

Walking In The Word Prayer

life, I rebuke any unnecessary fear, doubt, or sin in my life. In addition, I repent of all of my known and unknown sins, forgive myself and others, getting rid of all unwanted soul ties, yokes, or bondage, in the Name of Jesus.

As I strive to walk in the Spirit of Excellence and according to Your Word, let Your Holy Spirit refresh, guide, nudge, and renew my Spirit in ONENESS. My Way Maker, for You, are my refuge and fortress; fill me with Your Everlasting Peace that surpasses all understanding, allowing me to remain steadfast amid the Cycles, Seasons, and Vicissitudes of Life.

Father, I know everything is not all about me, so I also pray for those around me as You keep them in perfect peace. Lord, may Your Divine Light shine through me, touching or healing the hearts and minds of my family, friends, coworkers, or anyone who crosses my path. Lord, in a world that often seems unrestrained and divided, I seek Your Divine Intervention to bring Divine Harmony, Compassion, and Comfort to the hearts of all men. Lord, with the Divine Uplifting Power You have placed within me:

- ☐ I lift up those who are suffering from the consequences of conflict.
- ☐ I lift up those who are weak, sick, or frail.
- ☐ I lift up those who are hurting, wounded, or traumatized.
- ☐ I lift up those who are displaced, rejected, or homeless.
- ☐ I lift up those who are hungry, tired, or malnourished.
- ☐ I lift up those who are lost, abandoned, or confused.
- ☐ I lift up those who are hopeless, faithless, or doubtful.
- ☐ I lift up those who are enduring the wrath of another.
- ☐ I lift up those who are oppressed, yoked, or soul-tied.

I lift all of them in the Name of Jesus, advocating for those who cannot advocate for themselves and those in need.

Walking In The Word Prayer

In bridging the gap of love and understanding, I seek the Divine Call of Unity from the Ancient of Days; I lift up a prayer for the Leaders of our Nations. My Lord, my Heavenly Father, the Creator of us all, grant them Divine Wisdom and Compassion, that they may strive for justice and equality for all people, feeding Your precious sheep. While simultaneously prioritizing diplomacy over conflict and understanding over division, fostering peace and cooperation, and inspiring their citizens to do likewise, setting aside grudges and grievances. Father, the All-Sufficient One, please help our Leaders foster relationships that are rooted in RESPECT and EMPATHY one towards another, becoming slow to anger and quick to listen as a PEACEMAKER among the Nations.

As I do my part in *Walking in the Word*, let my actions, words, thoughts, and desires reflect Your Heavenly Love and Grace, and may others see You through me as I make a conscious decision to use the Fruits of the Spirit faithfully and consistently. As I walk in Your Word, use me as an instrument of peace, mercy, compassion, and understanding as You help me to encourage and uplift those who may be struggling, reminding them of the hope we have in You.

Also, in living abundantly, *As It Pleases You*, please allow me to become a conduit of Your Divine Blessings, as You have indeed Blessed me to be a Blessing to another, in the Name of Jesus. As I seek to experience Heaven on Earth, may my life be a Testament of Your Divine Goodness while trusting that all things are working together for my good. Thank You, Lord, for hearing my prayer, *Spirit to Spirit*, with Your UNENDING MERCY. I lift my voice in praise and say, Glory to the Highest! And peace on earth to all men, in the Mighty Name of Jesus, who is my Lord and Savior. In Your Holy Name, I pray. Amen.

Throne Room 24

Spiritual Echoes Prayer

Father, my God, my Creator, the *Spiritual Echoes* from the Heavenly of Heavens speak loudly, transcending to Earth with Spiritual Truths and Absolutes. I pray that every element of my life is under the subjection of the Holy Spirit, guiding, protecting, and leading me in the Name of Jesus.

As the *Spiritual Echoes* from the depths of my soul wail for the *Spirit to Spirit* Union between us, I humbly come before Your Heavenly Courts with honor and praise. Thus, for my highest and best use, *As It Pleases You*, I need Your Divine Mercy and Intervention to ensure that Kingdom Standards are met accordingly.

Father, I am the Salt of the Earth, and I will NOT lose my savor, nor will I allow my words, thoughts, attitudes, actions, and beliefs to become unseasoned, thrown out, or trampled. By Divine Decree, through the Wisdom of the Holy of Holies, everything that I think, everything I say, everything I do, and everything I become will be seasoned, accepted, and utilized, *As It Pleases You*, as You guide me in being a positive influence on those I interact with, those I randomly encounter on my Spiritual Journey, and those of whom I am assigned to.

My God, I am reminded of the importance of loving others unconditionally, even those who may be difficult to love. Help me to show kindness and compassion to everyone, regardless of my *Spiritual Echoes*, differences, secret traumas, or

Spiritual Echoes Prayer

disagreements, as You strengthen me to overcome any form of negativity, resentment, or animosity from within.

My loving and merciful Father, from the Heavenly of Heavens, Your *Spiritual Echoes* reveal my strengths and weaknesses to ensure that I remain on the correct path and steadfast in You. For this reason, I trust in Your Divine Provisions and Predestined Blueprint because You do not make mistakes, not now and not ever.

Hence, my Heavenly Father, on this day, I ask, seek, and knock, trusting in Your Infinite Wisdom and Boundless Love. I will not be consumed by worry, fear, or doubt, examining myself first and becoming self-aware, recognizing my own faults before pointing out the faults of others.

Lord, I need You, my perfect and loving Father. I also need the presence of the Holy Spirit and the Blood of Jesus to anoint the Spiritual Echoes from within. My Father in Heaven, help me to guard my heart and mind against evil thoughts and negative chatter while assisting me in reversing them from negative to positive, bad to good, and wrong to right.

And being that I cannot add a single moment to my life without You, I will move forward with You at the forefront in the Spirit of Excellence, Faith, Hope, and Courage, *As It Pleases You* with wisdom, mercy, compassion, fairness, and understanding. I trust in Your Divine Sovereignty, knowing that You care for every detail of my life, especially when I Spiritually Till, Grow, Multiply, and Share my own ground according to my Predestined Blueprint.

In this Throne Room, *As It Pleases You*, I surrender all, using all of the Spiritual Weapons given for my Spiritual Crops to yield. I know that it is only a TEST, symbolically TRAINING me to Grow Great in You, my Heavenly Father.

- ☐ In this Throne Room, I put on the Weapon of Confidence, Courage, and Stamina.

Spiritual Echoes Prayer

- ☐ In this Throne Room, I put on the Weapon of Expectation, Empathy, and Exhortation.

- ☐ In this Throne Room, I put on the Weapon of Optimism, Anticipation, and Vitality.

- ☐ In this Throne Room, I put on the Weapon of Hopefulness, Faith, and Trust.

- ☐ In this Throne Room, I put on the Weapon of Cheerfulness, Patience, Proactiveness, and Positivity.

- ☐ In this Throne Room, I put on the Weapon of Happiness, Joy, Love, and Peacefulness.

- ☐ In this Throne Room, I put on the Weapon of Lovability, Compassion, and Kindness.

- ☐ In this Throne Room, I put on the Weapon of Self-Control, Self-Mirroring, Self-Analysis, and Self-Correction.

In this Throne Room, I am receiving the desires of my heart. I am receiving all the good in my life. I am receiving BLESSINGS and FAVOR in my life.

As Your Divine Echoes reverberate through the Earth, shaking its foundation, I heed to Your Voice, taking nothing for granted. O Lord, I hear You, I hear them, I hear myself, and I hear it...whatever it is, let the Spirit of the Lord rise on HIGH, telling me whatever I need to know with whomever or about whatever, whenever, wherever, however, and whyever.

My Heavenly Father, with the Spiritual Echoes bellowing from the Ancient of Days, I am Your REVERED SERVANT on a Divine Mission, hearing what needs to be heard, seeing what needs to be seen, and downloading from the Heavenly of Heavens for a time such as this, delivering accurate and relevant MESSAGES. And, by the Blood of the Lamb, the Mediator of it all, I cover my HEAD to the SOLES of my feet with the Redemptive Power and the Spiritual Seals of The Heavenly Throne Room. With this Divine Covering, EVERY room that I step into, I step in with a LEGION of Angels with Flaming Swords that have been ASSIGNED to protect me from all hurt, harm, malice, danger, or ambushments.

From this day forward, I will not be distracted by the wiles of the enemy, nor will I become one. I am embracing my Tree of Life that will yield much fruit...GOOD FRUIT, to be exact. For this, my LEAVES will become the Healing Force to the NATIONS, healing the land for Your Holy Prophets, while I keep Your WORD to the Letter to enter into the Gates as the Bride of Christ, taking my SEAT at the Table. For this, O Lord, I trust and surrender to You, my Heavenly Father, in the Name of Jesus. Amen.

The Spiritual Seal for the Echoes

"But you have come to Mount Zion and to the city of the living God, the heavenly Jerusalem, to an innumerable company of angels, to the general assembly and church of the firstborn who are registered in heaven, to God the Judge of all, to the spirits of just men made perfect, to Jesus the Mediator of the new covenant, and to the blood of sprinkling that speaks better things than that of Abel. See that you do not refuse Him who speaks. For if they did not escape who refused Him who spoke on earth, much more shall we not escape if we turn away from Him who speaks from heaven, whose voice then shook the earth; but now He has promised, saying, 'Yet once more I shake not only the earth, but also Heaven.'" Revelation 12:22-26.

Spiritual Echoes Prayer

Asking the Spiritual Echoe Questions

Can the Spiritual Echoes speak? Absolutely. All you need to do is ask questions, listen, and learn. Why must a Believer query the Spiritual Echoes? If one does not do it for themselves, then who will do it for them? No one can query God for the exact details of the Divine Spiritual Echoes relating to our Predestined Blueprint outside of the one who has it on the Tablet of their Heart. Although glimpses are allowed, receiving Divine Instructions is not. It is a Spiritual Violation with enforceable penalties, similar to breaking into a bank, but in the Realm of the Spirit.

On the other hand, if we do not know about Spiritual Violations, the enemy will try to lay claim to our STUFF due to Spiritual Cluelessness. Then again, we cannot place a Spiritual Demand on what we do not understand. Nor can we demand Recompense on violations that we do not know about or are currently engaged in. So, in *The Asking Echoes*, when in the Throne Room, we can gain Spiritual Leverage by questioning, learning as we go, or awakening the Spirit Man from within, *As It Pleases God*.

Why do we need *The Asking Echoes*? It allows the enemy to underestimate us, causing them to get caught in their own warranted traps without us lifting a finger or cursing our own hands with debauchery. Really? Yes, really! The Kingdom Echoes are loud, profound, and potent! And those who do not know about the Spiritual Echoes from the Heavenly of Heavens will most often GET GOT due to their lack of understanding or preparedness. Is this fair? Absolutely!

Whatever we need is already, so we must do our homework, period! In school, can we pass without doing homework? The answer is no...we can try to beat the system,

Spiritual Echoes Prayer

but omitting the basics of learning makes us weak from the classroom to the pews and from the pews to the pulpit, erecting walls of codependencies while pretending to be independent.

No pun is intended, but those who DO NOT work on themselves, *As It Pleases God*, are known for their rotten fruits without realizing they are rotten while appearing right in their own eyes. Meanwhile, affecting others with their low-level, below-the-belt antics that are UNPLEASING to God, causing them to get a Spiritual Side-Eye.

A few of the most POWERFUL GIFTS to mankind are hidden within the ability to ask, seek, find, receive, understand, document, extract, and convert. If you opt out of asking questions, you will find yourself struggling in the areas of communication, unable to resolve issues, or having a constant battle with fallacies.

When dealing with the Spiritual Echoes in the Kingdom, AS KING, you must perfect the art of ASKING. Why? They are related in the Kingdom. In the same way that Jesus asked relevant questions, so should you. If not, you will become outsmarted by those who perfect their art of diverting, dodging, projecting, pitching, contorting, and snitching. Here is how to use it in The Throne Room, *As It Pleases God*, but not limited to such:

- ☐ The Spiritual Echoes are saying and asking: *"You are the salt of the earth, but if the salt loses its flavor, how shall it be seasoned? It is then good for nothing but to be thrown out and trampled underfoot by men."* Matthew 5:13.

Spiritual Echoes Prayer

- ☐ The Spiritual Echoes are asking: "*For if you love those who love you, what reward have you? Do not even the tax collectors do the same?*" Matthew 5:46.

- ☐ The Spiritual Echoes are saying: "*Therefore, I say to you, do not worry about your life, what you will eat or what you will drink; nor about your body, what you will put on. Is not life more than food and the body more than clothing?*" Matthew 6:25.

- ☐ The Spiritual Echoes are saying: "*Look at the birds of the air, for they neither sow nor reap nor gather into barns; yet your heavenly Father feeds them. Are you not of more value than they?*" Matthew 6:26.

- ☐ The Spiritual Echoes are asking: "*Which of you, by worrying, can add one cubit to his stature?*" Matthew 6:27.

- ☐ The Spiritual Echoes are saying and asking: "*Now if God so clothes the grass of the field, which today is, and tomorrow is thrown into the oven, will He not much more clothe you, O you of little faith?*" Matthew 6:30.

- ☐ The Spiritual Echoes are saying: "*Therefore do not worry, saying, 'What shall we eat?' or 'What shall we drink?' or 'What shall we wear?'*" Matthew 6:31.

- ☐ The Spiritual Echoes are asking: "*How can you say to your brother, 'Let me remove the speck from your eye'; and look, a plank is in your own eye?*" Matthew 7:4.

- ☐ The Spiritual Echoes are asking: "*Or what man is there among you who, if his son asks for bread, will give him a stone? Or*

Spiritual Echoes Prayer

if he asks for a fish, will he give him a serpent?" Matthew 7:9-10.

☐ The Spiritual Echoes are asking: *"Why are you fearful, O you of little faith?"* Matthew 8:26.

☐ The Spiritual Echoes are asking: *"Why do you think evil in your hearts?"* Matthew 9:4.

☐ The Spiritual Echoes are asking: *"Do you believe that I am able to do this?"* Matthew 9:28.

☐ The Spiritual Echoes are asking: *"Are not two sparrows sold for a copper coin? And not one of them falls to the ground apart from your Father's will."* Matthew 10:29.

☐ The Spiritual Echoes are asking: *"But to what shall I liken this generation?"* Matthew 11:16. Simply put, "To what can I compare this generation?"

☐ The Spiritual Echoes are asking: *"What man is there among you who has one sheep, and if it falls into a pit on the Sabbath, will not lay hold of it and lift it out?"* Matthew 12:11.

☐ The Spiritual Echoes are asking: *"If Satan casts out Satan, he is divided against himself. How then will his kingdom stand?"* Matthew 12:26.

☐ The Spiritual Echoes are asking: *"Brood of vipers! How can you, being evil, speak good things? For out of the abundance of the heart, the mouth speaks."* Matthew 12:34.

Spiritual Echoes Prayer

- ☐ The Spiritual Echoes are asking: "*Who is My mother and who are My brothers?*" Matthew 12:48.

- ☐ The Spiritual Echoes are asking: "*O you of little faith, why did you doubt?*" Matthew 14:31.

- ☐ The Spiritual Echoes are asking: "*Why do you also transgress the commandment of God because of your tradition?*" Matthew 15:3.

- ☐ The Spiritual Echoes are asking: "*Are you still so dull?*" Matthew 15:16.

- ☐ The Spiritual Echoes are asking: "*Don't you see that whatever enters the mouth goes into the stomach and then out of the body?*" Matthew 15:17.

- ☐ The Spiritual Echoes are saying and asking: "*But Jesus, being aware of it, said to them, "O you of little faith, why do you reason among yourselves because you have brought no bread? Do you not yet understand, or remember the five loaves of the five thousand and how many baskets you took up? Nor the seven loaves of the four thousand and how many large baskets you took up? How is it you do not understand that I did not speak to you concerning bread?—but to beware of the leaven of the Pharisees and Sadducees.*" Matthew 16:8-11.

- ☐ The Spiritual Echoes are asking: "*For what profit is it to a man if he gains the whole world, and loses his own soul? Or what will a man give in exchange for his soul?* Matthew 16:26.

- ☐ The Spiritual Echoes are asking: "*What do you think? If a man has a hundred sheep, and one of them goes astray, does he not

Spiritual Echoes Prayer

leave the ninety-nine and go to the mountains to seek the one that is straying?" Matthew 18:12.

☐ The Spiritual Echoes are asking: "*Should you not also have had compassion on your fellow servant, just as I had pity on you?*" Matthew 18:33.

☐ The Spiritual Echoes are asking: "*So He said to him, 'Why do you call Me good? No one is good but One, that is, God. But if you want to enter into life, keep the commandments.'* " Matthew 19:17.

☐ The Spiritual Echoes are asking: "*And about the eleventh hour he went out and found others standing idle, and said to them, 'Why have you been standing here idle all day?'* " Matthew 20:6.

☐ The Spiritual Echoes are asking: "*Are you able to drink the cup that I am about to drink, and be baptized with the baptism that I am baptized with?'* " Matthew 20:22.

☐ The Spiritual Echoes are asking: "*What do you want Me to do for you?*" Matthew 20:32.

☐ The Spiritual Echoes are asking: "*How did you come in here without a wedding garment?*" Matthew 22:12.

☐ The Spiritual Echoes are asking: "*Why do you test Me, you hypocrites?*" Matthew 22:18.

☐ The Spiritual Echoes are asking: "*For which is greater, the gold or the temple that sanctifies the gold?*" Matthew 23:17.

Spiritual Echoes Prayer

☐ The Spiritual Echoes are asking: "*How can you escape the condemnation of hell?*" Matthew 23:33.

☐ The Spiritual Echoes are asking: "*Do you think that I cannot now pray to My Father, and He will provide Me with more than twelve legions of angels?*" Matthew 26:53.

☐ The Spiritual Echoes are asking: "*How then would the Scriptures be fulfilled that say it must happen in this way?*" Matthew 26:54.

☐ The Spiritual Echoes are asking: "*Why do you reason about these things in your hearts?*" Mark 2:8.

☐ The Spiritual Echoes are asking: "*Which is easier, to say to the paralytic, 'Your sins are forgiven you,' or to say, 'Arise, take up your bed and walk'?*" Mark 2:9.

☐ The Spiritual Echoes are asking: "*Is it lawful on the Sabbath to do good or to do evil, to save life or to kill?*" Mark 3:4.

☐ The Spiritual Echoes are asking: "*How can Satan cast out Satan?*" Mark 3:23.

☐ The Spiritual Echoes are asking: "*To what shall we liken the kingdom of God? Or with what parable shall we picture it?*" Mark 4:30.

☐ The Spiritual Echoes are asking: "*Why are you so fearful? How is it that you have no faith?*" Mark 4:40.

Spiritual Echoes Prayer

☐ The Spiritual Echoes are asking: "*Who touched my clothes?*" Mark 5:30.

☐ The Spiritual Echoes are asking: "*Why make this commotion and weep?*" Mark 5:39.

☐ The Spiritual Echoes are asking: "*Are you thus without understanding also? Do you not perceive that whatever enters a man from outside cannot defile him, because it does not enter his heart but his stomach, and is eliminated, thus purifying all foods?*" Mark 7:18-19.

☐ The Spiritual Echoes are asking: "*How many loaves do you have?*" Mark 8:5.

☐ The Spiritual Echoes are asking: "*Why does this generation seek a sign?*" Mark 8:12.

☐ The Spiritual Echoes are asking: "*Do you see anything?*" Mark 8:23.

☐ The Spiritual Echoes are asking: "*Who do men say that I am?*" Mark 8:27.

☐ The Spiritual Echoes are asking: "*But who do you say that I am?*" Mark 8:29.

☐ The Spiritual Echoes are asking: "*Why then is it written that the Son of Man must suffer much and be rejected?*" Mark 9:12.

☐ The Spiritual Echoes are asking: "*What are you discussing with them?*" Mark 9:16.

Spiritual Echoes Prayer

- ☐ The Spiritual Echoes are asking: *"How long shall I be with you? How long shall I bear with you? Bring him to Me."* Mark 9:19.

- ☐ The Spiritual Echoes are asking: *"What was it you disputed among yourselves on the road?"* Mark 9:33.

- ☐ The Spiritual Echoes are asking: *"What did Moses command you?"* Mark 10:3.

- ☐ The Spiritual Echoes are asking: *"You do not know what you ask. Are you able to drink the cup that I drink, and be baptized with the baptism that I am baptized with?"* Mark 10:38.

- ☐ The Spiritual Echoes are asking: *"Was it from heaven or from men? Answer Me."* Mark 11:30.

- ☐ The Spiritual Echoes are asking: *"Why do you test Me?"* Mark 12:15.

- ☐ The Spiritual Echoes are asking: *"Are you not therefore mistaken, because you do not know the Scriptures nor the power of God?"* Mark 12:24.

- ☐ The Spiritual Echoes are asking: *"How is it that the scribes say that the Christ is the Son of David?"* Mark 12:35.

- ☐ The Spiritual Echoes are asking: *"Let her alone. Why do you trouble her? She has done a good work for Me."* Mark 14:6.

- ☐ The Spiritual Echoes are asking: *"Where is the guest room in which I may eat the Passover with My disciples?"* Mark 14:14.

Spiritual Echoes Prayer

- [ ] The Spiritual Echoes are asking: "*Are you sleeping? Could you not watch one hour?*" Mark 14:37.

- [ ] The Spiritual Echoes are asking: "*Are you still sleeping and resting? It is enough! The hour has come; behold, the Son of Man is being betrayed into the hands of sinners.*" Mark 14:41.

- [ ] The Spiritual Echoes are asking: "*Have you come out, as against a robber, with swords and clubs to take Me?*" Mark 14:48.

- [ ] The Spiritual Echoes are asking: "*Why did you seek Me? Did you not know that I must be about My Father's business?*" Luke 2:49.

- [ ] The Spiritual Echoes are asking: "*Why are you reasoning in your hearts?*" Luke 5:22.

- [ ] The Spiritual Echoes are asking: "*Which is easier, to say, 'Your sins are forgiven you,' or to say, 'Rise up and walk'?*" Luke 5:23.

- [ ] The Spiritual Echoes are asking: "*Is it lawful on the Sabbath to do good or to do evil, to save life or to destroy?*" Luke 6:9.

- [ ] The Spiritual Echoes are asking: "*If you love those who love you, what credit is that to you?*" Luke 6:32.

- [ ] The Spiritual Echoes are asking: "*If you lend to those from whom you hope to receive back, what credit is that to you?*" Luke 6:34.

Spiritual Echoes Prayer

- [ ] The Spiritual Echoes are asking: *"Can the blind lead the blind? Will they not both fall into the ditch?"* Luke 6:39.

- [ ] The Spiritual Echoes are asking: *"Why do you call Me 'Lord, Lord,' and not do the things which I say?* Luke 6:46.

- [ ] The Spiritual Echoes are asking: *"What did you go out into the wilderness to see? A reed shaken by the wind?"* Luke 7:24.

- [ ] The Spiritual Echoes are asking: *"What did you go out to see? A man clothed in soft garments?"* Luke 7:25.

- [ ] The Spiritual Echoes are asking: *"But what did you go out to see? A prophet?"* Luke 7:26.

- [ ] The Spiritual Echoes are asking: *"To what then shall I liken the men of this generation, and what are they like?"* Luke 7:31.

- [ ] The Spiritual Echoes are asking: *"When they had nothing with which to repay, he freely forgave them both. Tell Me, therefore, which of them will love him more?"* Luke 7:42.

- [ ] The Spiritual Echoes are asking: *"Where is your faith?"* Luke 8:25.

- [ ] The Spiritual Echoes are asking: *"What is your name?"* Luke 8:30.

- [ ] The Spiritual Echoes are asking: *"So which of these three do you think was neighbor to him who fell among the thieves?"* Luke 10:36.

- [ ] The Spiritual Echoes are asking: *"If a son asks for bread from any father among you, will he give him a stone? Or if he*

Spiritual Echoes Prayer

asks for a fish, will he give him a serpent instead of a fish? Or if he asks for an egg, will give him a scorpion?" Luke 11:11-12.

☐ The Spiritual Echoes are asking: "*If I cast out demons by Beelzebub, by whom do your sons cast them out?*" Luke 11:19.

☐ The Spiritual Echoes are saying and asking: "*You foolish people! Did not the one who made the outside make the inside also?*" Luke 11:40.

☐ The Spiritual Echoes are asking: "*Are not five sparrows sold for two copper coins? And not one of them is forgotten before God.*" Luke 12:6.

☐ The Spiritual Echoes are asking: "*Man, who made Me a judge or an arbitrator over you?*" Luke 12:14.

☐ The Spiritual Echoes are asking: "*Who will get what you have prepared for yourself?*" Luke 12:20.

☐ The Spiritual Echoes are asking: "*If you then are not able to do the least, why are you anxious for the rest?*" Luke 12:26.

☐ The Spiritual Echoes are asking: "*Who then is that faithful and wise steward, whom his master will make ruler over his household, to give them their portion of food in due season?*" Luke 12:42.

☐ The Spiritual Echoes are asking: "*Do you suppose that I came to give peace on earth? I tell you, not at all, but rather division.*" Luke 12:51.

Spiritual Echoes Prayer

- [ ] The Spiritual Echoes are saying and asking: "*Hypocrites! You can discern the face of the sky and of the earth, but how is it you do not discern this time?*" Luke 12:56.

- [ ] The Spiritual Echoes are asking: "*Do you not judge what is right?*" Luke 12:57.

- [ ] The Spiritual Echoes are asking: "*Do you suppose that these Galileans were worse sinners than all other Galileans, because they suffered such things?*" Luke 13:2.

- [ ] The Spiritual Echoes are asking: "*Do you think that they were worse sinners than all other men who dwelt in Jerusalem?*" Luke 13:4.

- [ ] The Spiritual Echoes are asking: "*Why does it use up the ground?*" Luke 13:7.

- [ ] The Spiritual Echoes are asking: "*Does not each one of you on the Sabbath loose his ox or donkey from the stall, and lead it away to water it?*" Luke 13:15.

- [ ] The Spiritual Echoes are asking: "*Then should not this woman, a daughter of Abraham, whom Satan has kept bound for eighteen long years, be set free on the Sabbath day from what bound her?* Luke 13:16.

- [ ] The Spiritual Echoes are asking: "*What is the kingdom of God like? What shall I compare it to?*" Luke 13:18.

- [ ] The Spiritual Echoes are asking: "*Suppose one of you wants to build a tower. Will he not first sit down and estimate the cost to see if he has enough money to complete it?*" Luke 14:28.

Spiritual Echoes Prayer

- [ ] The Spiritual Echoes are asking: "*What woman, having ten silver coins, if she loses one coin, does not light a lamp, sweep the house, and search carefully until she finds it?*" Luke 15:8.

- [ ] The Spiritual Echoes are asking: "*Therefore if you have not been faithful in the unrighteous mammon, who will commit to your trust the true riches?*" Luke 16:11.

- [ ] The Spiritual Echoes are asking: "*And if you have not been faithful in what is another man's, who will give you what is your own?*" Luke 16:12.

- [ ] The Spiritual Echoes are asking: "*Which of you, having a servant plowing or tending sheep, will say to him when he has come in from the field, 'Come at once and sit down to eat?'*" Luke 17:7.

- [ ] The Spiritual Echoes are asking: "*But will he not rather say to him, 'Prepare something for my supper, and gird yourself and serve me till I have eaten and drunk, and afterward you will eat and drink?*" Luke 17:8.

- [ ] The Spiritual Echoes are asking: "*Would he thank the servant because he did what he was told to do?*" Luke 17:9.

- [ ] The Spiritual Echoes are asking: "*Were there not any found who returned to give glory to God except this foreigner?*" Luke 17:18.

- [ ] The Spiritual Echoes are asking: "*And shall God not avenge His own elect who cry out day and night to Him, though He bears long with them? I tell you that He will avenge them speedily.*

Spiritual Echoes Prayer

Nevertheless, when the Son of Man comes, will He really find faith on the earth?" Luke 18:7-8.

- ☐ The Spiritual Echoes are asking: *"Why then did you not put my money in the bank, that at my coming I might have collected it with interest?"* Luke 19:23.

- ☐ The Spiritual Echoes are asking: *"What then is this that is written: 'The stone which the builders rejected Has become the chief cornerstone?' "* Luke 20:17.

- ☐ The Spiritual Echoes are asking: *"For who is greater, he who sits at the table, or he who serves? Is it not he who sits at the table? Yet I am among you as the One who serves."* Luke 22:27.

- ☐ The Spiritual Echoes are asking: *"When I sent you without a money bag, knapsack, and sandals, did you lack anything?"* Luke 22:35.

- ☐ The Spiritual Echoes are asking: *"Are you betraying the Son of Man with a kiss?"* Luke 22:48.

- ☐ The Spiritual Echoes are asking: *"Have you come out, as against a robber, with swords and clubs?"* Luke 22:52.

- ☐ The Spiritual Echoes are asking: *"For if men do these things when the tree is green, what will happen when it is dry?"* Luke 23:31.

- ☐ The Spiritual Echoes are asking: *"Why are you troubled? And why do doubts arise in your hearts?"* Luke 24:38.

Spiritual Echoes Prayer

- ☐ The Spiritual Echoes are asking: "*What does your concern have to do with Me? My hour has not yet come.*" John 2:4.

- ☐ The Spiritual Echoes are asking: "*Are you the teacher of Israel, and do not know these things?*" John 3:10.

- ☐ The Spiritual Echoes are asking: "*If I have told you earthly things and you do not believe, how will you believe if I tell you heavenly things?*" John 3:12.

- ☐ The Spiritual Echoes are asking: "*Will you give me a drink?*" John 4:7.

- ☐ The Spiritual Echoes are asking: "*Do you want to get well?*" John 5:6.

- ☐ The Spiritual Echoes are asking: "*How can you believe, who receive honor from one another, and do not seek the honor that comes from the only God?*" John 5:44.

- ☐ The Spiritual Echoes are asking: "*If you do not believe his writings, how will you believe My words?*" John 5:47.

- ☐ The Spiritual Echoes are asking: "*Where shall we buy bread, that these may eat?*" John 6:5.

- ☐ The Spiritual Echoes are asking: "*Does this offend you?*" John 6:61.

- ☐ The Spiritual Echoes are asking: "*Do you also want to go away?*" John 6:67

- ☐ The Spiritual Echoes are asking: "*Have I not chosen you?* John 6:70.

Spiritual Echoes Prayer

- ☐ The Spiritual Echoes are asking: "*Where are those accusers of yours? Has no one condemned you?*" John 8:10.

- ☐ The Spiritual Echoes are asking: "*Why do you not understand My speech? Because you are not able to listen to My word.*" John 8:43.

- ☐ The Spiritual Echoes are asking: "*Which of you convicts Me of sin? And if I tell the truth, why do you not believe Me?*" John 8:46.

- ☐ The Spiritual Echoes are asking: "*Do you believe in the Son of God?*" John 9:35.

- ☐ The Spiritual Echoes are asking: "*Many good works I have shown you from My Father. For which of those works do you stone Me?*" John 10:32.

- ☐ The Spiritual Echoes are asking: "*Where have you laid him?*" John 11:34.

- ☐ The Spiritual Echoes are asking: "*Did I not say to you that if you would believe you would see the glory of God?*" John 11:40

- ☐ The Spiritual Echoes are asking: "*Now My soul is troubled, and what shall I say? 'Father, save Me from this hour'? But for this purpose, I came to this hour.*" John 12:27.

- ☐ The Spiritual Echoes are asking: "*Do you understand what I have done for you?*" John 13:12.

Spiritual Echoes Prayer

☐ The Spiritual Echoes are asking: *"Will you lay down your life for My sake?"* John 13:38.

☐ The Spiritual Echoes are asking: *"Whom are you seeking?"* John 18:4.

☐ The Spiritual Echoes are saying and asking: *"Put your sword away! Shall I not drink the cup the Father has given me?"* John 18:11.

☐ The Spiritual Echoes are asking: *"Why do you ask Me? Ask those who have heard Me what I said to them. Indeed, they know what I said."* John 18:21.

☐ The Spiritual Echoes are asking: *"If I have spoken evil, bear witness of the evil; but if well, why do you strike Me?"* John 18:23

☐ The Spiritual Echoes are asking: *"Are you speaking for yourself about this, or did others tell you this concerning Me?"* John 18:34.

☐ The Spiritual Echoes are asking: *"Why are you weeping? Whom are you seeking?* John 20:15.

☐ The Spiritual Echoes are asking: *"Do you love me? He said to Him, 'Yes, Lord; You know that I love You.' He said to him, 'Tend My sheep.' "* John 21:16

☐ The Spiritual Echoes are asking: *"If I want him to remain until I return, what is that to you? You must follow me."* John 21:22.

Spiritual Echoes Prayer

Please note that these Spiritual Echoes provide insight into Jesus' teachings and the challenges He presented to his followers. And still, we are facing these same challenges and issues today.

So, the question is, 'What is the problem?' The problem is that we are not providing answers to these simple, yet profound questions. Until we do, we will continue the same cycle of déjà vu.

From the Ancient of Days until now, it behooves you to get into your Throne Room, *As It Pleases God*, and get to questioning yourself, *Spirit to Spirit*.

Throne Room References

Each reference contains nuggets of Divine Wisdom. Please allow the Holy Spirit to ILLUMINATE the story that fits your day. Why do we need a *Throne Room Glance*? Each story in the Bible contains a Spiritual Principle hidden in plain sight; however, every Spiritual Principle may not be applicable at every stage in our lives. Thus, we need the Holy Spirit to guide us and the Blood of Jesus to cover us amid whatever, whenever, however, wherever, and with whomever.

When connecting *Spirit to Spirit* in the Throne Room, write the Lesson Learned from each person, situation, circumstance, or event. Here is the Throned Roadmap:

- ☐ A Benediction (Priestly Blessing) — Numbers 6:24-26
- ☐ A Good Report — Numbers 1:19-33
- ☐ A Holy People — Deuteronomy 7:6-11
- ☐ A Kingdom of Priests — Exodus 19:3-6
- ☐ A Levite and his Concubine — Judges 19
- ☐ A Man Stoned on Sabbath Day — Numbers 15:32-36
- ☐ A Message for Esau — Genesis 32:1-20
- ☐ A Murderer — Leviticus 24:7
- ☐ A Night to Remember — Exodus 12:43-48
- ☐ A Plea for the People — Numbers 14:1; 10-25
- ☐ A Prophet Promised — Deuteronomy 18:17-19
- ☐ A Rebellious Son — Deuteronomy 21:18-21
- ☐ A Stubborn People — Deuteronomy 9:27-29
- ☐ A Symbol of Agreement — Genesis 31:38-55
- ☐ A Vain People — Deuteronomy 32:15-39
- ☐ A Vow of a Nazarite — Numbers 6:1-20
- ☐ A Wife for Isaac (Rebekah) — Genesis 24

Throne Room References

- [ ] Aaron Appointed Priest — Exodus 28:1
- [ ] Abner Goes Over to David — II Samuel 3:6-21
- [ ] Abraham and Isaac's Faith Tested — Genesis 22
- [ ] Abraham Deceives Pharaoh — Genesis 13
- [ ] Abraham Pleads with God — Genesis 16:16-33
- [ ] Abraham's Journey (The Call) — Genesis 12
- [ ] Abraham's Vision (The Promises) — Genesis 15
- [ ] Absalom returns to Jerusalem — II Samuel 14
- [ ] Absalom's Conspiracy — II Samuel 15:1-12
- [ ] Absalom's Death — II Samuel 18:1-18
- [ ] Achan's Punishment — Joshua 7:24-26
- [ ] Achan's Sin of Accursed Things — Joshua 7:1-23
- [ ] Achish Sends David Back to Ziklag — I Samuel 29
- [ ] Adam and Eve — Genesis 2
- [ ] Adam and Eve's Fall — Genesis 3
- [ ] Adam's Descendants — Genesis 5:1-32
- [ ] Advice of Hushai and Ahitophel — II Samuel 16:15-23; 17
- [ ] Alter at Mount Ebal — Deuteronomy 27:1-9
- [ ] Amalekites Attack the Canaanites — Numbers 14:45
- [ ] Amnon and Tamar — II Samuel 13
- [ ] Amorite kings defeated — Joshua 10:1-11
- [ ] An Act of Revenge — Genesis 34
- [ ] Angel of the Lord at Bokim — Judges 2:1-5
- [ ] Anointment Instruction — Exodus 30:25:26
- [ ] Appointment of Spies — Numbers 13:1-3
- [ ] Ark Brought to Jerusalem — II Samuel 6
- [ ] Ark in Ashdod and Ekron — 1 Samuel 5
- [ ] Ark of the Covenant — Exodus 25:1-22
- [ ] Ark Returned to Israel — 1 Samuel 6-7:2
- [ ] As a Man Disciplines His Son — Deuteronomy 8:5
- [ ] Ascension of Jesus — Acts 1
- [ ] Atonement for Sin — Exodus 32:30-35
- [ ] Atonement for Unsolved Murder — Deuteronomy 21:1-14
- [ ] Baby Moses — Exodus 2
- [ ] Balaam Blesses Israel — Numbers 24:1-9

Throne Room References

- ☐ Balaam prophesied about Jesus — Numbers 24:17-20
- ☐ Balaam's ass spoke to Him — Numbers 22:15-35
- ☐ Baptism of Jesus — Matt. 3:13; Mark 1:9; Luke 3:21
- ☐ Battle of Jericho — Joshua 6
- ☐ Battle with Amorites — Numbers 21:21-32
- ☐ Beatitudes — Matt. 5:3-12
- ☐ Beware of Idol Worship — Deuteronomy 8:11-20
- ☐ Birth of Isaac — Genesis 21:1-8
- ☐ Birth of Ishmael — Genesis 16
- ☐ Birth of Jesus — Luke 2
- ☐ Birth of Joseph — Genesis 30:22:24
- ☐ Birth of Moses — Exodus 1:15-22, 2:1-25
- ☐ Birth of Samson — Judges 13:1-25
- ☐ Birth of Samuel — 1 Samuel 1:1-20
- ☐ Blasphemy Punished — Leviticus 24:10-16
- ☐ Blessings for Obedience — Deuteronomy 28:1-14
- ☐ Blessings or Curses — Deuteronomy 22-31
- ☐ Boaz Marries Ruth — Ruth 4:1-12
- ☐ Book of the Law — Deuteronomy 31:9-13
- ☐ Borders of the Promised Land — Numbers 34:1-12
- ☐ Bread of Heaven — Exodus 16
- ☐ Bridled Tongue — James 3
- ☐ Burning Bush — Exodus 3
- ☐ Burnt Offering — Exodus 29:10-26
- ☐ Cain and Abel (The First Murder) — Genesis 4:1-15
- ☐ Cain's Family — Genesis 4:16-24
- ☐ Captain of the Host of the Lord — Joshua 5:13-15
- ☐ Care for Widows — Deuteronomy 24:17-22
- ☐ Circumcise Your Heart — Deuteronomy 10:16
- ☐ Cloud and Fire — Numbers 9:15-22
- ☐ Coming of the Holy Spirit — Acts 2
- ☐ Complaints Against Moses — Exodus 17:1-6
- ☐ Confession of Guilt — Leviticus 5:1-5
- ☐ Consecration Service — Exodus 29:1-9
- ☐ Conversion of Saul (Paul) — Acts 9

Throne Room References

- ☐ Courage of Battle — Deuteronomy 20
- ☐ Covenant Renewed at Mount Ebal — Joshua 8:30-35
- ☐ Creation of Man — Genesis 2:7
- ☐ Creation — Genesis 1
- ☐ Crossing of River Jordon — Joshua 3-4
- ☐ Crossing of the Red Sea — Exodus 14
- ☐ Crucifixion — Matt. 27:15-54; Mark 15:24; Luke 23:33
- ☐ Curses of Disobedience — Deuteronomy 27:9-26, 28:13-48
- ☐ Daniel in the Lion's Den — Daniel 6
- ☐ Danites settle in Laish — Judges 18
- ☐ Darkness Over the Land — Exodus 10:21-29
- ☐ David Again Spares Saul's Life — I Samuel 24
- ☐ David Again Spares Saul's Life a 2nd Time — I Samuel 26
- ☐ David Among the Philistines — I Samuel 28
- ☐ David and Bathsheba — II Samuel 11
- ☐ David and Goliath — I Samuel 17
- ☐ David and Jonathan — I Samuel 20
- ☐ David and Mephibosheth — II Samuel 9
- ☐ David and Ziba — II Samuel 16:1-14
- ☐ David Anointed King Over Judah — II Samuel 2:1-7
- ☐ David at Adullam and Mizpah — I Samuel 22:1-5
- ☐ David at Gath — I Samuel 21:10-15
- ☐ David at Nob — I Samuel 21:1-9
- ☐ David Became King Over Israel — II Samuel 5:1-5
- ☐ David Conquers Jerusalem — II Samuel 5:6-16
- ☐ David Defeats the Ammonites — II Samuel 10
- ☐ David Defeats the Philistines — II Samuel 2:17-25
- ☐ David Destroys the Amalekites — I Samuel 30
- ☐ David Flees Absalom — II Samuel 15 to 17
- ☐ David Heard of Saul's Death — II Samuel 1:1-16
- ☐ David Mourns Death of Absalom — II Samuel 18:19-33; 19
- ☐ David Saves Keilah — I Samuel 23:1-6
- ☐ David Spares Saul's Life — I Samuel 24
- ☐ David, Nabal, and Abigail — I Samuel 25
- ☐ David's Lament — II Samuel 1:17-27

Throne Room References

- [ ] David's Officials — II Samuel 8:15-18
- [ ] David's Prayer — II Samuel 7:18-29
- [ ] David's Psalm of Thanksgiving — II Samuel 22
- [ ] David's Victories — II Samuel 8:1-7
- [ ] Days of Unleavened Bread — Exodus 13:6-10
- [ ] Dealing with Jealousy — Numbers 5:11-31
- [ ] Death in the Land — Exodus 12:29-32
- [ ] Death of Aaron — Numbers 20:23-29
- [ ] Death of Abraham — Genesis 25
- [ ] Death of Egyptian Cattle — Exodus 9:1-7
- [ ] Death of Eli — 1 Samuel 4:12-22
- [ ] Death of Isaac — Genesis 35:27-29
- [ ] Death of Jacob — Genesis 49:33, 50:1-6
- [ ] Death of Joseph — Genesis 50:22-26
- [ ] Death of Joshua — Joshua 24:28-31
- [ ] Death of Moses — Deuteronomy 34
- [ ] Death of Samson — Judges 16:23-31
- [ ] Deborah — Judges 4:1-24
- [ ] Description of the Altar — Exodus 27
- [ ] Destroy All Idols — Deuteronomy 12:2-3
- [ ] Destruction by Fire — Genesis 19:23-26
- [ ] Dinah Defiled — Genesis 34
- [ ] Disobedience and Defeat — Judges 2:6-23; 3:1-5
- [ ] Disobedience of Aaron's Sons — Leviticus 10:1-4; 16:1-4
- [ ] Division of the Promised Land — Numbers 34:13-29
- [ ] Divorce Procedure — Deuteronomy 24:1-4
- [ ] Do not Add To or Diminish the Word of God — Deut. 12:32, Prov. 30:6, and Rev. 22:18-19
- [ ] Do not question God's Work — Number 12, 16
- [ ] Draw near to God — James 4:8
- [ ] Eli's Wicked Sons — 1 Samuel 2:12-26
- [ ] Elijah and the Prophets of Baal — I Kings 18
- [ ] Esau sells his Birthright — Genesis 25:29-34
- [ ] Esau's Descendants — Genesis 36:9-12
- [ ] Esau's Hatred for Jacob — Genesis 27:41-45

Throne Room References

- ☐ Exclusion From the Assembly — Deuteronomy 23:1-7
- ☐ Ezekiel's Vision of Cherubim — Ezekiel 10
- ☐ Faith and Works — James 2
- ☐ Fall of Jericho — Joshua 5:13-15; 6:1-27
- ☐ False Worship — Leviticus 20:1-8
- ☐ Families of the Tribes of Israel — Numbers 26
- ☐ Family Vows — Numbers 30
- ☐ Fasting — Matthew 6:16-18
- ☐ Feast Days — Leviticus 23:27-41, Deuteronomy 16:13-22
- ☐ Feast unto God — Exodus 23:14-17
- ☐ Feasts of the Lord — Leviticus 23:4-10
- ☐ Fed by Quail — Numbers 11:13, 31-33
- ☐ Feeding of the Thousand — Luke 9
- ☐ Fiery Furnace — Daniel 3
- ☐ First Fruits and Tithes — Deuteronomy 26:1-15
- ☐ First Time Moses Struck the Rock — Exodus 17:5-6
- ☐ Five Amorite Kings Killed — Joshua 10:16-28
- ☐ Follow Commandments — Deuteronomy 26:16-19
- ☐ Fruits of the Spirit — Galatians 5:22-23
- ☐ Gad and Reuben's Choice — Numbers 32:1-37
- ☐ Garments of the Priest — Exodus 28:4-30
- ☐ Genealogy of David — Ruth 4:13-22
- ☐ Gibeonite Deception — Joshua 9:1-27
- ☐ Gideon — Judge 6 to 8
- ☐ Gideon Defeats the Midianites — Judges 7:1-25
- ☐ Glory of the Lord — Leviticus 9:23-24
- ☐ God Leads the People — Exodus 13:21-22, 14:1-14
- ☐ God Meet Balaam — Numbers 23:1-26
- ☐ God Rescues Israel from Egypt — Exodus 12
- ☐ God send an Angel unto You — Exodus 23:20-23
- ☐ God Showed Moses the Promised Land — Numbers 28:12
- ☐ God spoke to Israel (Jacob) — Genesis 46:2-4
- ☐ God spoke to Jacob — Genesis 35:1-15
- ☐ God spoke to Moses — Exodus 6:28-30, 7:1-19

Throne Room References

- ☐ God spoke to the Children of Israel   Exodus 19:9-25, 20:1-19
- ☐ God was disappointed that the People Cried, Wept, and Murmured   Numbers 14:1-45
- ☐ God's anger with the Children   Deuteronomy 1:34-46
- ☐ God's Call to Abram   Genesis 12
- ☐ God's Chastisement   Leviticus 26:14-39
- ☐ God's Instructions to Judges   Deuteronomy 1:16-18
- ☐ God's Instructions to the Children Of Israel about the Promised Land   Numbers 33:50-56
- ☐ God's Mighty Acts   Deuteronomy 11:1-7
- ☐ God's Powerful Voice   Exodus 19:3-25; 20; 21; 22; 23; 24; 26 Deuteronomy 5
- ☐ God's Promise to David   II Samuel 7:1-17
- ☐ God's Promise to Moses   Genesis 4
- ☐ God's Promise to Noah   Genesis 9:8-17
- ☐ God's Promise to Sarah   Genesis 18:9-15
- ☐ God's Punishment   Numbers 14:26-35
- ☐ God's Work of Creation   Genesis 1
- ☐ God's wrath   Deuteronomy 28:15-29
- ☐ Golden Calf   Exodus 32:15-28
- ☐ Golden Rule   Matthew 7
- ☐ Good Samaritan   Luke 10
- ☐ Growth of the Church   Book of Acts
- ☐ Hagar the Maidservant and Ishmael   Genesis 16
- ☐ Hagar and Ishmael Sent Away   Genesis 21:9-21
- ☐ Hail Mixed with Fire   Exodus 9:18-35
- ☐ Hannah Dedicates Samuel   1 Samuel 1:21-28
- ☐ Hannah's Prayer   1 Samuel 2:1-11
- ☐ He Is the Rock   Deuteronomy 32:4-13
- ☐ I am Joseph, Your Brother   Genesis 45:1-11
- ☐ I Am the Lord, Their God   Exodus 29:46
- ☐ Idol Worship Forbidden   Exodus 23:24
- ☐ Idols Forbidden   Leviticus 26:1-4
- ☐ Instructions for Warfare   Deuteronomy 20:15-20

Throne Room References

- [ ] Invasion of Locusts — Joel 1:1-12
- [ ] Isaac and Rebekah — Genesis 24
- [ ] Ish-Bosheth Murdered — II Samuel 4
- [ ] Israel Asked for a King — 1 Samuel 8
- [ ] Israel Defeated — Deuteronomy 1:41-46
- [ ] Israel Fights the Remaining Canaanites — Judges 1:1-36
- [ ] Israel Without Weapons — 13:16-22
- [ ] Israel's Rebellion Predicted — Deuteronomy 31:14-29
- [ ] Israelites Committed Sins of Idolatry — Numbers 25:1-9
- [ ] Israelites Fight the Benjamites — Judges 20
- [ ] Jacob addresses His Sons — Genesis 48:1-32
- [ ] Jacob and Esau — Genesis 25:21-34
- [ ] Jacob and Esau Reconciled — Genesis 33:1-11
- [ ] Jacob deceives Isaac — Genesis 27:15-46
- [ ] Jacob Grieves for Joseph — Genesis 37:31-35
- [ ] Jacob Plans for a Journey — Genesis 31:11-18
- [ ] Jacob Prospers — Genesis 30:37-43
- [ ] Jacob Visits Laban — Genesis 28:10
- [ ] Jacob was renamed to Israel — Genesis 32:27-28
- [ ] Jacob Wrestles with an Angel — Genesis 32
- [ ] Jacob's Dream — Genesis 28:10-15
- [ ] Jacob's Love for Rachel — Genesis 29:10-30
- [ ] Jacob's Sons — Genesis 29:32-35, 30:12-24
- [ ] Jacob's Vision of the Ladder — Genesis 28
- [ ] Jesus and the Children — Mark 10
- [ ] Jesus and Zacchaeus — Luke 19
- [ ] Jesus Clears the Temple — Luke 2
- [ ] Jesus Stills the Storm — Mark 4
- [ ] Jesus talks with Nicodemus — John 3
- [ ] Jesus walks on Water — John 6
- [ ] Jethro Advises Moses — Exodus 18
- [ ] Joab Murders Abner — II Samuel 3:22-39
- [ ] Job's Prosperity Restored — Job 42
- [ ] John's Revelation at Patmos — Book of Revelation
- [ ] Jonah and the Big Fish — Jonah 1

Throne Room References

- ☐ Jonathan Attacks the Philistines — 1 Samuel 13:23; 14:1
- ☐ Joseph Brothers went to Egypt — Genesis 42, 43
- ☐ Joseph Buries His Father — Genesis 50:7-13
- ☐ Joseph changed Unjustly — Genesis 39:1-19
- ☐ Joseph Dies in Egypt — Genesis 50:22-26
- ☐ Joseph explains a Dream — Genesis 40
- ☐ Joseph explains Pharaoh's Dream — Genesis 41:25-41
- ☐ Joseph in Prison — Genesis 39:20-23
- ☐ Joseph revealed Himself — Genesis 45:1-8
- ☐ Joseph sends for Jacob (His Father) — Genesis 45:9-21
- ☐ Joseph Two Sons — Genesis 41:50-52
- ☐ Joseph was rewarded by Pharaoh — Genesis 41:42-47
- ☐ Joseph's Brothers Sold Him — Genesis 37:25-36
- ☐ Joseph's Dream — Genesis 37:5-11
- ☐ Joseph's Emergency Plan — Genesis 47:13-28
- ☐ Joseph's Family in Egypt — Genesis 46:8-34
- ☐ Joseph's Family Settles in Goshen — Genesis 47:1-12
- ☐ Joseph's Jealous Brothers — Genesis 37:13-24
- ☐ Joseph's Promise to His Father — Genesis 47:29-31
- ☐ Joshua Chosen to Lead the Israelites — Numbers 27:15-23
- ☐ Joshua Strategy Against Ali — Joshua 8:1-30
- ☐ Joshua to Succeed Moses — Deuteronomy 31:1-8
- ☐ Jubilee Observance — Leviticus 25:8-22
- ☐ Judah and Tamar — Genesis 38:7-30
- ☐ Judah Pleads with Joseph — Genesis 44
- ☐ Judge Fairly — Deuteronomy 17 1-13
- ☐ Just Treatment of the Poor — Exodus 22:25
- ☐ Korah's Punishment — Numbers 16:15-40
- ☐ Korah's Rebellion — Numbers 16:1-14
- ☐ Laban Searches the Camp — Genesis 19-35
- ☐ Land Redemption — Leviticus 25:23-34
- ☐ Last Supper — Matthew 26
- ☐ Laws about Property — Exodus 22:5-6
- ☐ Laws Concerning Servants — Exodus 21
- ☐ Lazarus Raised from the Dead — John 11

Throne Room References

- ☐ Let My People Go — Exodus 5
- ☐ Life and Death — Deuteronomy 30:15-20
- ☐ Life in the Garden of Eden — Genesis 2
- ☐ Life of Jesus — Matthew, Mark, Luke & John
- ☐ List of Defeated Kings — Joshua 12
- ☐ Lord appeared unto Abraham — Genesis 18
- ☐ Lord Calls Samuel — 1 Samuel 3
- ☐ Lord Commands Joshua (Promised Land) — Joshua 1
- ☐ Lord is God — Deuteronomy 4:29-40
- ☐ Lord of Lord — Deuteronomy 10:17-22
- ☐ Lord Rejected Samuel as King — 1 Samuel 15
- ☐ Lord's Prayer — Matthew 6
- ☐ Making of the Ark — Exodus 37:1-9
- ☐ Man shall not live by Bread Alone — Deuteronomy 8:3
- ☐ Marital Guidelines — Deuteronomy 22:13-30
- ☐ Melchizedek meets Abraham — Genesis 14:18
- ☐ Micah's Idols — Judges 17
- ☐ Miracle of Water into Wine — John 2
- ☐ Miscellaneous Laws — Deuteronomy 23:15-25
- ☐ Moses Alone with God — Exodus 34:1-29
- ☐ Moses Blesses the Tribes — Deuteronomy 33:1-29
- ☐ Moses Blesses the Tribes — Deuteronomy 33
- ☐ Moses in the Tabernacle — Exodus 33:9-23
- ☐ Moses Instruct the people — Exodus 35
- ☐ Moses Makes an Offering — Exodus 24:1-8
- ☐ Moses on Mount Sinai — Exodus 19:9-25
- ☐ Moses saw God — Exodus 24:9-18
- ☐ Moses struck the Rock — Numbers 20:2-13
- ☐ Moses Views Promised Land — Deuteronomy 32:48-52
- ☐ Naomi and Ruth — Ruth 1; 2
- ☐ Nathan Rebukes David — II Samuel 12
- ☐ Noah and the Ark (Flood) — Genesis 6
- ☐ Noah's Descendants — Genesis 10
- ☐ Northern Kings Defeated — Joshua 11
- ☐ Nothing but Manna — Numbers 11:1-13

Throne Room References

- ☐ Offering for Ignorance — Numbers 15:22-31
- ☐ Ornaments of Worship — Exodus 25:23-40
- ☐ Parable of the Dry Bones — Ezekiel 37
- ☐ Passover Observance — Numbers 9:1-12, Deuteronomy 16:1-7
- ☐ Peter's Denial — Luke 22
- ☐ Peter's Sermon — Acts 3
- ☐ Pharaoh Refuses to Listen — Exodus 10:1-2
- ☐ Pharaoh's Army Destroyed — Exodus 14:24-29
- ☐ Philip Talks with an Ethiopian — Acts 8
- ☐ Philistines Capture the Art — 1 Samuel 4:1-11
- ☐ Philistines Subdued at Mizpah — 1 Samuel 7:2:17
- ☐ Plague and Despair — Deuteronomy 28:59-68
- ☐ Plague of Blood — Exodus 7:14-24
- ☐ Plague of Boils — Exodus 9:8-12
- ☐ Plague of Darkness — Exodus 10:21-29
- ☐ Plague of Flies — Exodus 8:20-32
- ☐ Plague of Frogs — Exodus 8:1-15
- ☐ Plague of Gnats (Lice) — Exodus 8:16-19
- ☐ Plague of Hail — Exodus 9:13-35
- ☐ Plague of Locusts — Exodus 10:3-20
- ☐ Plague of the Camp — Numbers 16:41-50
- ☐ Plague on Livestock — Exodus 9:1-7
- ☐ Plague on the Firstborn — Exodus 11:1-12:36
- ☐ Preparation for Passover — Exodus 12 1-32
- ☐ Preparation for War — Numbers 25:16-18; 26:1-4
- ☐ Priest Robe — Exodus 28:31-35
- ☐ Prince of Peace — Isaiah 9
- ☐ Prodigal Son — Luke 15
- ☐ Promised Blessings — Leviticus 26:40-46
- ☐ Prophecy Against the House of Eli — 1 Samuel 2:27-36
- ☐ Prosperity After Turning to God — Deuteronomy 30:1-10
- ☐ Provision for the Poor — Deuteronomy 15:7-11
- ☐ Punishment for doing Wrong — Deuteronomy 11-21
- ☐ Quails and Manna — Exodus 16; Numbers 11

Throne Room References

- [ ] Queen of Sheba Visits Solomon — I Kings 10
- [ ] Rahab and the Spies — Joshua 2
- [ ] Reading of the Law — Deuteronomy 31:89-29
- [ ] Rebekah and Jacob Plot — Genesis 27
- [ ] Refused by Edom — Numbers 20:14-22
- [ ] Release of Bondmen or Slave — Deuteronomy 15:12-18
- [ ] Remember the Lord — Deuteronomy 9:18-20
- [ ] Renewal of the Covenant — Deuteronomy 29:1-14
- [ ] Resist Temptation — Deuteronomy 13:12-18
- [ ] Resurrection of Jesus — Luke 24
- [ ] Return of the Spies — Numbers 13:25-33
- [ ] Right of the Firstborn — Deuteronomy 21:15-17
- [ ] Rule by Nations — Deuteronomy 28:49-58
- [ ] Rules for Priests — Leviticus 21 & 22
- [ ] Ruth and Boaz on the Threshing Floor — Ruth 3
- [ ] Ruth and Naomi — Ruth 1
- [ ] Ruth Meets Boaz — Ruth 2
- [ ] Sabbath Observance — Exodus 31:12-17
- [ ] Samson and Delilah — Judges 16:1-22
- [ ] Samson's Marriage — Judges 14
- [ ] Samson's Vengeance on the Philistines — Judges 15
- [ ] Samuel and Eli — I Samuel 3
- [ ] Samuel Anoints David — 1 Samuel 16
- [ ] Samuel Anoints Saul — 1 Samuel 9 & 10
- [ ] Samuel Farwell Speech — 1 Samuel 12
- [ ] Samuel Rebukes Saul — 1 Samuel 13:1-15
- [ ] Sarah's Death — Genesis 23
- [ ] Saul Confirmed as King — 1 Samuel 11:12-15
- [ ] Saul Family — 1 Samuel 14:49-52
- [ ] Saul Kills the Priests of Nob — 1 Samuel 22:6-23
- [ ] Saul Made King — 1 Samuel 10:9-27
- [ ] Saul Pursues David — 1 Samuel 23:7-29
- [ ] Saul rescues the City of Jabesh — 1 Samuel 11:1-11
- [ ] Saul Takes His Life — 1 Samuel 31
- [ ] Saul Tries to Kill David — 1 Samuel 19

Throne Room References

- [ ] Saul's Jealousy of David — 1 Samuel 18
- [ ] Sermon on the Mount — Matthew 5:1-7:29
- [ ] Serpents Bit the Israelis — Numbers 21:1-9
- [ ] Sexual Behavior — Leviticus 18
- [ ] Sexual Purity — Leviticus 20:10-23
- [ ] Sheba Rebels Against David — II Samuel 20
- [ ] Sin's Consequences — Genesis 3:13-24
- [ ] Soft Answer — Proverbs 15
- [ ] Solomon Becomes King — I Kings 1:28-32
- [ ] Solomon Builds the Temple — I Kings 6
- [ ] Solomon's Wisdom — I Kings 3
- [ ] Song of Deborah — Judges 5:1-31
- [ ] Song of Moses — Exodus 15:1-19, Deut. 32:1-43
- [ ] Southern Cities Conquered — Joshua 10:29-43
- [ ] Spies Saved by Rahab — Joshua 2:1-23
- [ ] Spilling Seed of Onan — Genesis 38:8-10
- [ ] Stealing — Deuteronomy 24:7
- [ ] Stiff-necked People — Deuteronomy 9:6-29
- [ ] Story of Lot — Genesis 19
- [ ] Strong Drink Forbidden — Leviticus 10:8:12
- [ ] Stubborn and Rebellious Son — Deuteronomy 21:18-21
- [ ] Sun Stood Still — Joshua 10:12-15
- [ ] Sustained by Manna — Exodus 16:11-35
- [ ] Tabernacle Described — Exodus 26
- [ ] Tabernacle Duties — Numbers 4:1-33
- [ ] Tabernacle Filled with God's Glory — Exodus 40:33-38
- [ ] Teach Your Children — Deuteronomy 6:6-25
- [ ] Temptation and Sin — Genesis 3:1-13
- [ ] Temptations of Jesus — Matthew 4; Mark 1; Luke 4
- [ ] Ten Commandments — Exodus 20, Deuteronomy 5:6-21
- [ ] Thou Shall Not... — Leviticus 19
- [ ] Tithe — Leviticus 27:30-32
- [ ] Tithe for the Levites — Numbers 18:25-32
- [ ] Tower of Babel — Genesis 11
- [ ] Towns for the Levites — Joshua 21:1-45

Throne Room References

- ☐ Transfiguration of Jesus on the Mount — Matthew 17
- ☐ Treatment of the Poor — Leviticus 25:35-46
- ☐ Triumphal Entry into Jerusalem — John 12
- ☐ Two Angels visit Lot — Genesis 19:1-30
- ☐ Uncleanness in the Camp — Deuteronomy 23:9-14
- ☐ Unleavened Bread — Leviticus 6:16-18
- ☐ Various Laws — Deuteronomy 22:1-12
- ☐ Victory Assured — Deuteronomy 7:16-26
- ☐ Victory Over Amalek — Exodus 17:8-16
- ☐ Victory Over Midian — Numbers 31:1-18
- ☐ Victory Over Og — Deuteronomy 3:1-11
- ☐ Vow of a Nazarite — Numbers 6:2-20
- ☐ War Between the House of David And Saul — II Samuel 2:8-32; 3:1-5
- ☐ Water covers the Earth — Genesis 7
- ☐ What does God require of You — Deuteronomy 10:12-13
- ☐ Wilderness Murmuring — Exodus 15:24-27
- ☐ Wisdoms and Her Rewards — Proverbs 8
- ☐ Witches and Wizards — Leviticus 20:27
- ☐ Wives for the Benjamites — Judges 21
- ☐ Woman at the Well — John 4
- ☐ Writing on the Wall — Daniel 5

www.ingramcontent.com/pod-product-compliance
Lightning Source LLC
Chambersburg PA
CBHW071415160426
43195CB00013B/1697